A lawyer-turned-writer, **Mallika Ravikumar** writes and curates content on Indian history, law, culture and nature. She has been published by Penguin, Hachette, and Karadi Tales, amongst others. In her spare time, she is learning about trees, conducting tree walks, or sharing tree-stuff on her YouTube channel, *Tree Talk with Mallika Ravikumar*—from tree identifying tips, to myths and legends about them. You can find out more about her books, tree walks and history talks, at www.mallikaravikumar.com, and reach her on Instagram at mallika.ravikumar and treetalkwithmallikaravikumar.

An
M4
MYSTERY
BOOK 1

THE CASE OF THE VANISHING GODS

MALLIKA RAVIKUMAR

talking CUB
An Imprint of Speaking Tiger Books

TALKING CUB
Published by Speaking Tiger Books LLP
125A, Ground Floor, Shahpur Jat,
Near Asiad Village, New Delhi - 110 049

Published in Talking Cub by Speaking Tiger Books in paperback in 2023

ISBN: 978-93-5447-649-5
eISBN: 978-93-5447-651-8

10 9 8 7 6 5 4 3 2 1

Typeset in Lora by Jojy Philip
Printed at HT Media Ltd, Greater Noida

To

the nameless sculptors of ancient India,
who breathed life into stone

'The rate and scale at which India's art heritage is simply vanishing should alarm you. It certainly shocks me. Conservative estimates peg the number of medium to large Indian antiquities looted at around one thousand per year. That means that on an average day, close to three important pieces are stolen and will likely disappear forever.'

—S. Vijay Kumar, *The Idol Thief; The True Story of the Looting of India's Temples*

Contents

1

Malhar

'Stolen!' whispered an animated voice from the doorway. 'Jewellery and cash. Worth nearly two crores!'

'What?' Aaji crossed the threshold and stepped into the porch. 'Where?'

'That old Shenoy couple,' the voice spoke again. 'In A3...'

Sprawled on a sofa in the living room, Malhar snapped shut the book in his hand and sat up, back straight, eyes wide, ears alert. He had been reading *The Mystery of the Burnt Cottage*, his favourite mystery novel, for the third time, and wondering if life would ever present him with an opportunity to solve the kind of mysteries that Fatty, Larry, Pip, Daisy and Bets cracked during their summer holidays. But nothing exciting ever happened in the back-of-beyond coastal town of Maulsari, where his dad had been posted five months ago. Even with the Senior Superintendent of Police for a father, and a practicing criminal lawyer for a mother, his life was as dull as history class. And now, all of a sudden, a mystery seemed to have come calling through the door!

'Do karod!' the voice gasped again. 'Even a hundred generations of my family haven't seen that kind of money, Maji!'

Jumping over the coffee table and couch, Malhar dashed like a bullet to the door. On the porch, Subhash chacha, the dhoti-clad raddiwala, who came by each fortnight to collect all kinds of scrap, was seated on his haunches beside a heap of newspapers.

'That's shocking!' Aaji clicked her tongue as she handed the man a stack of used milk packets.

'Could you please tell sahib to help?' asked Subhash chacha.

'The police will do whatever is necessary. I do not interfere in my son's work.'

'I do not mean it that way, Maji,' the old man smiled awkwardly, as Malhar stood leaning on the door-frame, head at a tilt, latching on to every word of the turbaned man. 'The police suspect the maid who was working for the Shenoys because she had their keys. Her name is Sarla and she's been detained for questioning. Poor Sarla is not at fault, Maji. She is my neighbour, I have known her for many years. She has three little children and a drunk scoundrel for a husband who earns nothing. Please Maji,' pleaded Subhash chacha with folded hands, 'please put in a good word for her. Do request sahib to go easy on Sarla. I can guarantee she is not involved.'

'I told you, I do not interfere in my son's work,' said Malhar's grandmother. 'How am I to know that this Sarla is innocent? The police will do their job. Don't you worry.'

Tying up the scrap, Chacha handed Aaji a ten-rupee note. Then, he bundled it all up tightly with a rope and placed it on his cycle outside the porch. 'Maji! I nearly forgot,' he turned around. 'I'm going to the gaon because my uncle passed away. I might not be back for two months.' Calling to a boy leaning on a tamarind tree outside, he continued, 'Mirchi here will come in my place to collect the kabaadi.'

'Mirchi!' Malhar snickered, sizing up the wiry boy in a tattered shirt with a scowling face. 'What a name!'

'This drumstick of a fellow?' Aaji beckoned him closer. 'Don't you get anything to eat?' she asked the boy, then turned to the old man. 'Does he know the job? Will he weigh the stuff correctly?'

'Don't you worry, Maji,' replied Subhash chacha. 'He's been collecting scrap since he was born. That is all he knows.' The old man turned his cycle around to leave.

'Wait,' Aaji turned to the kitchen and brought out two parathas wrapped in paper. 'Malhar beta, go get one of your shirts and give it to the boy.'

'Tch!' Ambling reluctantly to his room, Malhar returned with a green shirt he didn't much care for. 'Here,' he stepped outside and dangled it on an outstretched arm before Mirchi, then took a step back, hit by the boy's sweaty odour.

Taking it without a word, Mirchi walked away.

'What was he saying about some burglary, Aaji?' asked Malhar, closing the door behind him.

'A theft...in Urmila Shenoy's house,' said Aaji. 'With the SSP's bungalow in the colony, one would think it's a safe place but anything can happen these days. Just yesterday, in that *Crime Watch* serial, they showed —'

'And what was he saying about some maid and the police? Have they found the thief?'

'Not yet.' Aaji sank into an armchair and reached for the television remote. 'They suspect the maid because she had the house keys. But he says the lady is innocent. Who knows...these days nobody can be trusted...' she muttered, before tuning back to her favourite crime show.

Malhar stood still for a moment, his mind racing through the plot of every mystery book he'd read and re-read. He ran to the large bookshelf at the end of the corridor to look up burglary cases; then ransacked the smaller shelf in his own room. *Burglary. Maid. House Keys. Suspect.* He found no parallels. With a sigh, he threw himself on the bed. And then, as he lay there, staring blankly at the ceiling, a smile lit up his eyes.

A door had been thrown open and the life he yearned for had come storming in. He could see Fatty and Larry standing there, wishing him luck, egging him on to solve the Mystery of the Neighbourhood Burglary. He could finally live the life of his favourite characters! Malhar sat up with a start. The summer holidays had just begun; and it was promising to be anything but a dull vacation.

2

Meera

'You will not take me to your office again!' Meera chided her mother, bundling her wavy hair into a ponytail, shutting the door behind her.

'But I thought you were bored at home,' said Madhavi Pradhan, depositing the car keys on a tray by the door. 'Besides, you're almost fourteen now. There was a lot you could have learned if you'd paid attention at my client's meeting instead of playing some silly game on the computer.'

'Some factory worker has been fired...why should his life be of any interest to me? No thanks! I'd rather stay here and finish my jigsaw puzzle. Or just fight with this idiot.' She tapped Malhar on his head.

'There's been a burglary in our colony!' announced Malhar, his voice charged with excitement.

'Burglary!' Meera's eyes grew large. 'Where? When? How?'

'At that Shenoy couple's house,' said Aaji, tapping the pause button on the remote. 'In that A3 building,' she pointed vaguely towards a set of buildings to the east.

'Harsh Shenoy's parents?' gasped Madhavi Pradhan, sitting down beside her mother-in-law. Having moved into Maulsari only a few months ago, most residents of Customs Colony were strangers, or at best vague acquaintances. But they knew the Shenoys because they were amongst the most amiable and sociable residents of the large complex.

'What? Gilderoy Lockhart's house?' Meera turned to Malhar, referring to Harsh Shenoy by the name they'd given him, as he reminded them of the charming professor from Harry Potter.

'His parent's house,' Malhar pulled Meera into their room and shut the door. 'Aunty and uncle live one floor above Gilderoy Lockhart...I mean one floor above Harsh uncle and his family, in the same building. Their niece stays with them. Her name is Preeti. The burglary took place yesterday when Shenoy aunty and her husband had gone out in the afternoon. The police suspect Sarla, their maid who had their house keys. But Subhashji—the raddiwala chacha—he is sure it's not her,' Malhar paused to take a breath after rattling off the information he'd managed to collect from building watchmen in the hour since he'd heard the news.

'What is the matter with you?' Meera frowned, sitting on the window ledge, beside a table where she'd laid out a 5000-piece jigsaw puzzle of a forest scene. 'Why are you so excited?'

'Didi! This is our chance to be like the Find-outers! We can solve the mystery!' said Malhar, the veins on his neck throbbing with excitement.

'Huh?' Meera picked up a puzzle piece and looked for a suitable spot to place it. 'You want *us* to solve this case?'

'Why not? If the Famous Five can do it and the Five Find-outers can do it, why not us?'

'Ma says the two of us can't get through a meal together without an argument. And you want us to team up to solve a real case?' Meera shrugged, setting down the piece with the macaque's tail. 'Please, Malhar, don't talk rubbish! Let's just have lunch and go to art class. Ghosh aunty has asked us to come early today.'

'Hey!' Malhar stepped towards the window and pointed to the first of the two buildings opposite them. 'Ghosh aunty is in the same building! The theft took place on the second floor...art class is on the fourth floor.'

'So?'

'Didi, we can try and look for clues!' Malhar plonked himself before the puzzle. 'What's there to lose?'

Meera stared at Malhar and exhaled hard. With school closed and few friends in this drab town, neither of them had much to do. Given their father's crazy schedule, there was little prospect they'd be going anywhere on a summer holiday. And surely, it was a better idea than dusting shelves in her mother's office.

'Oh...c'mon, Didi! You can be Sherlock and I can be your Watson.'

'Of course!' Meera crossed her arms across her chest. 'You are too stupid to solve anything by yourself.'

The idea had begun to tempt her. Malhar let the jibe pass.

Meera eyed the books strewn about the bed. The journey had begun with Enid Blyton and her endearing little detectives, who spent their summer holidays solving all sorts of local crimes riding about in their cycles across the English countryside. Satyajit Ray's Feluda had come next, chasing down jewel thieves and pinning down smugglers alongside his cousin Topshe. Nancy Drew, the stylish sleuth, had followed, solving crimes solo as she raced about the big city in her car. With Agatha Christie's Hercule Poirot, she had set about looking for murderers. And finally, she had discovered the greatest of them all—Sir Arthur Conan Doyle's Sherlock Holmes and his able assistant Dr Watson. With them, she'd moved through mysterious moors, zipped down busy streets, chasing the cleverest of criminals. She stood up and picked up the books, inhaling the fragrance of their yellowed pages, running her fingers along their dog-eared corners. Secret missions and double agents. Encrypted codes and hidden clues. Buried treasures and mysterious murders. Exciting chases and lurking dangers. The prospect was thrilling;

the lure of the unknown beckoned; the call of adventure whispered.

'Alright!' Meera smiled, 'Let's do it!'

3

Mirchi

'Six!' All eyes travelled skyward as the ball flew across the grass and over a line of mast trees, to land amongst a row of bushes along the edge of the Dhyan Chand Maidan.

'Ball! Ball! Ball!' shouted the players, a signal to those at the periphery to retrieve the ball.

As the designated kacha-limbu, that job fell on Malhar's shoulders. Reluctantly, yet again, he went scampering to fetch the ball.

Sipping coconut water on a plastic chair under a clump of trees, Meera couldn't help wondering what joy her silly brother found in baking under the sun in the eternal hope that the big boys would give him a chance to bat. She turned to the blue diary on her lap, flipped it open and wrote:

Mystery of the Stolen Jewellery

Meanwhile, crawling on all fours, Malhar searched the undergrowth for the ball. 'Ouch ouch ouch!' he winced, pricked by a thorny shrub. But even as he slowed down to rub the gash on his arm and feel sorry for himself, another figure emerged from the bush, ball in hand. Malhar stared at the scraggy figure. It was the same drumstick fellow he'd seen earlier. 'What...uh... are you doing here?'

Mirchi threw the ball back and made no reply.

'Hey, I'm talking to you! What are you doing here?'

'Kyun?' Mirchi shot back. 'Is this your father's maidan?'

'So rude!' grumbled Malhar, and turned his attention to the game.

Resting his bottom on the parapet running along the ground's edge, Mirchi was immersed in the game. Malhar tried to focus on the match as well, but his eyes drifted constantly towards Mirchi, moving from the boy's torn rubber chappals, his bare lanky legs dotted with bruises, up his tattered shorts to his dirt-streaked face. He noticed the underside of Mirchi's nose caked with snot; his hair like an inverted bowl of dry hay over his head, and flies buzzing about a gaping wound on his elbow. The boy looked like he hadn't bathed in days.

'I live there,' Mirchi said suddenly, pointing to a row of shanties beyond the field. 'In Anand Nagar.'

'With Subhash chacha?'

'He's not my chacha-vacha. But haan, he lives close by.'

'By the way...' Malhar inched closer. 'You know Sarla?'

'Sarla?'

'The maid that Subhash chacha mentioned—the one who works in Shenoy aunty's house.'

Mirchi wasn't listening. The batting team needed 12 runs to win in 10 balls. The match was more exciting than some Sarla and Shenoy who didn't remotely concern him.

'Did she steal the jewels? Do you know?'

'Tereko kya hai?'

Malhar turned sideways to face Mirchi, noting the boy's interest in the game. 'You take me to where Sarla lives and I will give you a bat.'

Now Mirchi turned to face Malhar, disbelief in his eyes. Having never owned a bat, and with little hope of owning one, the prospect excited him immensely. 'A solid bat like Kohli,' he said, 'not those flimsy plastic ones of chhota bacchas.'

'Yes, yes!' nodded Malhar. 'A wooden bat like Kohli's. But you must take me to Sarla's house first.'

Mirchi beamed. He could not believe the deal he was getting. Back at Anand Nagar, Aslam bhai, the scrap dealer, bargained with him for every pound of junk he brought him. That too after he'd spent an entire day scavenging the streets for worthwhile junk. Even when he managed to get something stunning, like an unbroken pencil box or a complete picture frame, he seldom got a good bargain. But here he was, being offered a wooden bat for peanuts! What a good day, Mirchi chuckled to himself. 'After the match,' he turned up his nose, aware that his information was worth a price.

'Done!' Malhar smiled, pleased with himself for having sniffed out a beginning to the trail.

4

Munna

Making their way into a narrow alley opposite the maidan, Malhar and Meera followed Mirchi into Anand Nagar, staring uneasily at the closely clustered homes, each no more than a crude assembly of some bricks, corrugated tin, tarpaulin sheets and bamboo poles. A child peered at them from above a ladder on the left, a woman scrubbing plates outside a door looked up from a soapy puddle on the right. Making a rapid turn here, ducking under a clothesline there, they emerged onto an open patch under a large water tank. Three bare-footed children ran about in the middle, feral pigs and goats fed on a pile of garbage at one end, and a billboard rose at the other, with a bevy of filmstars on it, urging the people of Anand Nagar to simply toss a spoonful of paan masala into their mouth and experience the taste of success.

Standing under the tank, Mirchi stuck two fingers into his mouth. 'PHEEEEEE PHEEEEE PHEEEEE' he whistled thrice. In less than a minute, a black dog with white patches on his neck, sides and feet, came bounding towards him, and then began dancing around the boy.

'Dekh, Munna,' Mirchi bent down and threw his arms around the dog, 'I'm going to get a bat like Virat Kohli's,' he said, tugging Munna's ears. 'Now you wait and see, everyone will want to play with me.'

Meera looked on with a grin, as Munna licked Mirchi all over, then jumped about the two of them, tail wagging rapidly. Mirchi produced a biscuit from his pocket, then held it before Munna, who crunched it up as they walked on.

'Mirchi...kya tum,' Meera was about to ask if he lived nearby, but Mirchi cut in, compelled to make a point.

'I knowing the English,' said Mirchi. 'You speaking me English.'

'That's...uh...that's great!' Meera smiled awkwardly, even as Malhar winced at the sight of the filth floating on the nallah alongside, hit by an overpowering acrid smell.

'Daily I taking kachra patti from beauty parlours. All aunties there speaking English. So I knowing...' Mirchi offered an explanation, sauntering casually through the narrow lane, even as Malhar placed his feet carefully to avoid stepping into puddles, as the asphalt had made way for loose earth, stopping to check the underside of his shoes every now and then.

'That,' Mirchi stopped all of a sudden, pointing to a house at the end of a lane. 'Chilbil house.'

'Chilbil?'

'Sarla daughter.'

'You all have such funny names!' ginned Malhar.

'What you coming to see?' Mirchi raised an eyebrow.

'You've done what was necessary,' Malhar brushed the boy aside. 'The rest is none of your business.'

Meera fixed Malhar with a disapproving glare.

'When you giving me bat?' asked Mirchi.

'Meet me tomorrow morning at ten under the big banyan tree at the maidan,' said Malhar. 'I'll get it for you.'

Mirchi shrugged. 'But if you no come, I coming to your house. Remember, I knowing where you live,' he said, before turning away along with Munna.

'You didn't have to be so rude!' Meera admonished her brother as they approached the end of the lane. 'He is the one who got us here.'

'I got us here.' Malhar made big eyes. 'And I am going to give him a bat! Why do you want him to know what we're doing?' he said, as they spotted two women and two little girls, seated on a rope cot outside the last house.

Meera pulled Malhar behind a blue water drum.

'I am ruined!' one of the women was sobbing softly, 'Not only am I caught in this police enquiry, I have also lost my job. And nobody will give me a job now. What am I to do now? How do I feed my children?'

'That must be Sarla,' whispered Malhar. Sarla was speaking in Marathi, a language they could understand.

Meera fixed her brother with another stare. He had this annoying habit of stating the obvious. Peeping out she had a good look at the woman. She was demure and petite, dressed in a yellow synthetic saree, red bindi on her forehead, hair in a dishevelled bun, green glass bangles on her frail hands, a beaded mangalsutra strung around her neck. 'I don't know for what sins God is punishing me.'

She dabbed her face with the pallu of her saree, then pulled her daughters close and wiped their tears.

'The police say I must have known they had so much jewellery in the cupboard because they recently had a wedding in the family,' she said, banging her forehead violently with her palms. 'But if I wanted to steal, would I not have done it already? I have been working there for eleven years. I had their keys for the last eight years!'

'Here,' the other woman opened a newspaper packet and handed it to her. 'You mustn't have eaten anything since morning. Eat first...'

Sarla opened the packet and distributed the rotis to her children. The younger girl tapped her, then made some signs with her hand. The mother smiled slightly, replied with some more hand-signs, then took half a roti from the child's hand.

'The girl,' Malhar whispered again, 'she uh…she's…'

'Deaf…' Meera swallowed a lump in her throat.

'My good-for-nothing husband cares for nothing but his bottle. With great difficulty, I put these two in school,' wept Sarla, 'I didn't want them to have a miserable life like mine. But now I won't have enough to put food on their plates.'

Overcome with sympathy, Meera decided they'd done enough snooping for the day. She signalled to Malhar and they retreated quietly out of the alley.

'It's not Sarla,' mumbled Meera, as they tried finding their way back through the maze of tiny lanes.

'No,' Malhar nearly skipped, less bothered now by the mud and filth, pleased to find the number one police suspect in the clear. For that meant they had a mystery to solve!

5

Maulsari

'What if Sarla's husband did it?' whispered Malhar, gulping down his breakfast the next morning. 'He could have taken her keys and stolen the jewels. She may not know about it.'

Meera said nothing. Instead, she turned to her father who was behind the newspaper at the head of the table. 'Baba, are you investigating the Shenoy house theft?'

In the middle of his daily morning survey of every local newspaper, Senior Superintendent of Police Dhananjay Pradhan, made no reply.

'Baba!' Meera thumped her palms on the table. 'I'm talking to you!'

'Yes, beta,' Meera's father folded the paper and put it aside. 'What does my daughter want to know so eagerly this morning?'

'I asked if you are investigating the burglary at the Shenoy house.'

'Well, as the senior-most police officer in the district, every case that takes place in Maulsari is technically under me,' said SSP Pradhan, putting away his reading glasses and reaching for his tea. 'But I do not handle the investigation directly. The inspector in-charge of the local police station will be enquiring into this. Besides, such matters are official and confidential. Not breakfast-table chit-chat with children,' he smiled through his bushy moustache.

Malhar gave Meera an *I-told-you-so* stare. What was she expecting? Their father never discussed official matters at home, and did not appreciate any interference—neither from politicians, nor from family. Meera had been foolish to think otherwise.

'But Baba...' Meera probed on. 'Did the police find any clues?'

'We get no first-hand information even though we live with the SSP,' muttered Aaji from the couch as she watched the re-run of her favourite crime show.

'Baba, the newspapers say there was no break-in and that there were no fingerprints,' Meera persisted.

'I'm happy to know you've started reading the newspaper,' her father gave her a pat.

'Then it must have been a very clever thief. I don't think the poor house maid could have planned that.'

'My dear Sherlock!' smiled Meera's father, munching on a pear. 'I see you're concerned and excited about a neighbourhood burglary. But don't cross the line. Your summer holidays have begun—climb trees, go mango-picking, go to the beach, or hiking with friends.

Discover some interesting places around Maulsari. Let the police do their job and you do yours,' he said, roughing Malhar's curls affectionately, as he rose from the table.

'What friends?' grumbled Meera. 'It's been four months, and everyone still calls me *new-girl* at school.'

'And what interesting places?' mumbled Malhar. 'There's nothing to see in Maulsari! What a boring posting you're stuck with, Baba.'

'No place by the sea can be boring,' said the SSP. 'And Meera, don't you have a summer project about stepwells? The Rajmata Stepwell in the outskirts of Maulsari is one of the finest in the country. Why don't you go and see? I hear it is quite spectacular. Or go visit the prehistoric caves and the fort on the hill. I'm told the views are stunning. I wish I could do all this...and you both...you have all the time in the world and still won't go! There is much you can discover, if only you keep your eyes and mind open.' He turned towards the door as Constable Murli, the house orderly, gathered his lunch bag and briefcase. 'Madhavi, I can drop you on the way...you ready?' he called out to his wife.

'Coming coming,' Madhavi Pradhan emerged from her study, holding a stack of papers bound in red-cloth folders. 'By the way, Danny, speaking of that stepwell, you remember our history lecturer in college, Sahasrabudhe ma'am? I found out only last week that she is the director at the Stepwell Museum. On the pretext of Meera's school project, I would like to go and meet her. How about we go next week?' she suggested to the children, then fixed them with a kiss, waved to Aaji, and turned to the door.

Watching his parents leave, Malhar sat back with slumped shoulders. 'You go to that stupid stepwell and museum,' he frowned at his sister. 'I'm not coming! And now I have to take my bat to that drumstick-fellow,' he grunted, his eyes on the wall clock.

'I'll come with you,' said Meera. 'I want to talk to Mirchi.'

'Why?' Malhar scowled.

'He can help us,' Meera bunched her hair into a ponytail.

'What? Are you crazy? I'm not talking to him again... don't know when he had a bath!'

'Look, we need a partner who knows stuff that we don't.' Meera carried her plate into the kitchen. 'He led us to Sarla yesterday, didn't he? And as you said, we should check up on Sarla's husband too. Mirchi may be able to tell us more about him. And who knows, he may know Velu too!'

'Velu?' Malhar followed behind her. 'Now who the hell is this Velu?'

Meera turned to her brother, hand on her hip. 'Before you woke up this morning, I went out for a jog,' she said, turning back to rinse her cup and plate in the sink. 'Badal Singh—the watchman uncle—told me some plumber named Velu had visited Shenoy aunty's flat yesterday afternoon.'

'I've already given this Mirchi my shirt and now my bat,' Malhar exhaled hard, unimpressed by Meera's ideas. 'Yesterday I saw him looking at my watch. I'm telling you now, Didi, I'm not going to give him anything else!'

'Fine!' sighed Meera. 'Just pack some biscuits for Munna, will you? And leave the rest to me.'

6

M4

Malhar had three cricket bats. One was brand new and gleaming; the other, older, smaller and duller; and the third, overused, chipped on the side, with the rubber handle-encasement pealing. The third is what lay waiting on the grass beneath the banyan tree, as Malhar tried swinging from its thick aerial roots.

'My bat!' a delighted Mirchi came running towards the tree, dressed in his new green shirt, a cloth bag strung across his shoulder, Munna bounding behind him. Grabbing the bat even before Malhar could hand it over, he ran into the middle, raising it over his head like a trophy.

'He has no manners,' grunted Malhar. 'He didn't even say thank you!'

'Excellent shot by Virat Kohli over the covers,' announced Mirchi, pretending to smash a boundary. 'India ko chahiye 10 runs in 2 balls…AND… Wah! What a straight drive!' he shouted, posing with the straight face of the bat. 'Now India 6 runs needing…1 ball…only Kohli can do it!' He tapped the bat on the ground, preparing to take strike. 'That's a SIX! Kya baat hai! India has won! And a century for Kohli in thirty balls!' Mirchi raised his bat to acknowledge the applause from the imaginary crowds.

Meera laughed, enthralled by Mirchi's antics. Malhar found himself giggling, as he, too, often pretended to play with running commentary. Munna circled around them excitedly wagging his tail, as Mirchi came running towards them.

'Dost! I never forgetting you,' beamed Mirchi, smiling from ear to ear. 'This day...most happy day...in whole life.'

Malhar felt a goosebump or two on his arm, moved more by Mirchi's heartfelt emotions than a perfunctory *thank-you* could have ever conveyed. He smiled, surprised to see how much joy a broken bat had given their new friend.

'So...uh..' Meera pointed to a shack at the beach across from the maidan. 'Shall we go and have some juice?'

'Chal, Munna,' Mirchi turned the other way. 'Now Mirchi showing all peoples his bat. Then you seeing the masti. All peoples saying... Mirchi, I your friend!'

'Mirchi,' Meera said hesitantly, 'We want you to come with us.'

'Main?' Mirchi turned back, 'Juice ke liye?'

Meera nodded, rubbing Munna on the white underside of his neck.

Mirchi stared at her. Nobody had ever said such a thing to him before.

'You like juice or no?' asked Meera, unable to read his vacant expression.

'Arre baba…I no have money for juice-voose,' Mirchi wiggled his outstretched palm, baffled by the idea.

'That's okay. We'll pay.'

'Munna, dekh, aaj my lucky day!' Mirchi began his running commentary again, following Meera and Malhar towards the beach, Munna trotting by his side.

'So, why are you called Mirchi?' asked Meera as they walked.

'Big story!' Mirchi smiled. 'My sister name Nimbu, and I am Mirchi.'

'Nimbu Mirchi!' squealed Meera. 'Really? Like the nimbu-mirchi we hang for good luck?'

'Haan…wahich,' nodded Mirchi. 'My mother hanging nimbu-mirchi on door. My Dadi getting angry. She saying, why you wasting good nimbu and mirchi on door every day? So one day, she throwing away nimbu-mirchi and telling my mother we both enough for good luck. She no needing anything else. So from that day, my sister is Nimbu and I became Mirchi!'

'What a fun story,' Meera clapped. 'I wish I had a wacky name like that. So…what's your real name then?'

'My real name?' Mirchi scratched his head as they arrived at the juice shack. 'I no remember now! Everyone calling me Mirchi only…'

'At school also your name is Mirchi?' asked Meera, pulling up plastic chairs after placing their orders.

'I don't...' Mirchi hesitated. 'Meaning, I used to, but stopped going school...because other childrens making fun.'

'Making fun?' Meera squinted against the sunlight.

'Because, I Valmiki,' replied Mirchi matter-of-factly, eyeing the glass of watermelon juice with big eyes.

'Valmiki?' asked Malhar.

Mirchi stared at Malhar. 'You not knowing Valmiki?'

'Of course we know,' replied Meera, 'He composed the Ramayana.'

Head thrown back, hand on stomach, Mirchi had a hearty laugh. 'So, you not hearing about Valmiki caste?'

Meera shook her head.

'Valmiki is name of my caste,' Mirchi picked up his glass. 'Now no say me that you not knowing caste,' he paused and shot them an incredulous look. When they nodded he continued, 'My baap dada—all sweepers—so, other children in my school and some teachers also...they saying me, Mirchi, why you learning to read and write? When you grow up, you anyway becoming kachra-wala! I no like it when they say like that. I no like— ' Mirchi looked away, his smile quickly turning to a frown.

'Wait,' Meera leaned forward, remembering something from that client meeting her mother had had with the factory worker. 'There is a law. Atrocities law or something,' she tried recollecting. 'People cannot be nasty to you or mistreat you because of your caste. And...and...if they do, you can...' she snapped her fingers, trying to recall the advice her mother had given that worker. But she hadn't paid close attention. She couldn't remember. 'I'll find out and tell you,' she sat back. 'My mother is a lawyer....'

'Do you know Velu?' asked Malhar, keen to get on with the purpose of their meeting.

Sipping noisily from his glass, Mirchi shook his head.

'Can you help us find this plumber named Velu?' asked Meera, picking up her glass of kokum-sharbat.

'I don't know any Velu,' replied Mirchi. 'Kyun?'

'So,' Meera pulled her chair closer to the table. 'You must have heard of the burglary in our colony.'

Mirchi nodded.

'We are trying to solve the case. That's why we wanted you to take us to Sarla's house yesterday. But we found that she is not—'

'You helping that Dhurandhar Bhatawdekar to find chor?' squinted Mirchi.

Meera spat out the juice in her mouth and nearly choked. 'Helping who?'

'Father,' Mirchi corrected himself with an awkward smile. 'I mean your Baba...police...'

'What did you just call him?' Meera gaped at Mirchi.

'Arre, that board outside your house na. Your father name...' Mirchi tried to explain.

'Dhananjay Bhalerao Pradhan,' said Malhar, visibly offended. 'That's the board outside our house. It is our father's name.'

'Arre haan wahich! You see that old old movie—*Rang Birangi*—in that policeman with moustache like your father, his name Dhurandhar Bhatawdekar...and your board same to same so everyone calling your father like that.'

'It is *not* same to same...' grunted Malhar.

'Look who's talking! The boy who names people Snape and Voldemort!' Meera rolled her eyes at her brother, before turning back to Mirchi. 'That's so funny! Wait till Baba hears that,' she giggled, rubbing a gurgling Munna on his tummy. 'But no,' she added. 'We are not doing this for Baba. We want to solve the case on our own. Some plumber named Velu had visited Shenoy aunty's house just before the theft. So we wanted to check up. And we also want to know more about Sarla's husband. By the way,' said Meera, giving in to an impulsive idea, 'do you want to team up with us to solve this case?'

'Sachi muchi?' Mirchi's eyes turned large in surprise.

'Didi, what's wrong with you?' Malhar tugged at his sister's arm, his voice hushed, his eyes imploring. 'What are you doing?'

Meera fixed her brother with *I-know-what-I'm-doing* stare. Then she put her arms around Munna, 'What good are the Famous Five and Find-outers without a dog?' she smiled.

'There are two things I always wanted,' said Mirchi before Malhar could launch into another protest. 'A cricket bat like this,' he ran his hand over the blade of the bat. 'And to be policeman. Today you make both dreams real,' he beamed.

'Do you know you get dimples on both cheeks when you smile?' said Meera.

'No, my house...mirror broken,' Mirchi felt his cheeks with the tip of his fingers. 'So, I no seeing whole face.'

'You say such ridiculous things,' giggled Meera, drawing another glare and grunt from her brother. He couldn't see beyond the dirt on Mirchi's face; she, on the other hand, saw nothing beyond the twinkle in his eye. 'Actually, we could call ourselves the M4.'

'M4?' Mirchi scrunched his eyes, then they lit up with comprehension. 'Oh haan! Meera, Malhar, Munna aur Mirchi!' he slapped his hands together. 'Badhiya!'

'So, are we a team?' asked Meera.

'Arre haan haan,' grinned Mirchi. 'You knowing, my Dadi saying me, Mirchi, you going to be great man, someday! Who knows, if you with me...you both also becoming great!'

Meera laughed, Malhar grimaced.

Little did the M4 know then, that far from closing in on a case of theft, they were about to open up a can of worms.

7

From the Horse's Mouth

'Ask her na!' Malhar prodded his grandmother as they gravitated towards the frail lady on a marble platform by the entrance to the Devi Mandir.

'Tch,' Aaji clicked her tongue. She had just spent the last hour telling her grandson why it wasn't nice to poke their nose in other people's affairs. But as her eyes fell upon the forlorn woman, she couldn't hold back.

'Very sorry to hear about the theft at your home, Urmila-ji,' she said, zeroing in like a prey upon its quarry. 'I was shocked when I found out.'

Mrs Shenoy looked up from the little prayer book in her hand and smiled slightly, the strain showing on her face. And yet, she was well turned-out as always, dressed in a crisp cotton saree, her grey hair tied in a neat bun.

Keen to strike up a conversation, Meera and Malhar pressed their palms together. 'Namaste, aunty.'

'With god's grace, you will get it back,' Aaji turned to the Hanuman idol in a crevice on the right. 'If you don't mind, tell me one thing,' she plonked her stout frame on the marble ledge. 'Why did you keep so much jewellery at home and not in a bank locker?'

Meera winked at her brother; her bet on Aaji's innate curiosity was paying off, just as she'd predicted. She sat down by her grandmother, as Malhar crossed his legs and settled on the cool floor.

'They're usually in the bank locker,' Mrs Shenoy closed her prayer book. 'But we had a wedding in the family last week. And now this rathotsav next week...'

'Rathotsav?' whispered Malhar.

'It's a big annual event in our community,' Mrs Shenoy nodded. 'The temple idols are taken out in a chariot in a grand procession. Thousands gather for the event. It's very festive.'

A priest in a white dhoti appeared before them and pressed some petals and pedas into their palms, then wandered off to continue his distribution.

'I had taken out the jewels from the bank locker for my nephew's wedding,' Mrs Shenoy continued. 'I had planned to put them back the very next day. But my son Harsh said why not wait till after the rathotsav? He knows I find it difficult to climb up and down into the bank vault to access the locker. My knees are weak because of arthritis. So, to help me avoid two trips, he suggested we just keep the jewels locked in the safe at home till the rathotsav. It was a matter of one more week anyway,' she sighed, resting her head on the pillar behind her.

'Hmmm,' Aaji nodded sympathetically. 'The jewellery all in all, it's value must have been...' her voice trailed off.

'They were family heirlooms—my mother's kuteek—earrings set with nine diamonds,' said Mrs Shenoy, her hands instinctively moving to her ears. 'A precious necklace we call the vataana-haar that belonged to my late mother-in-law, kari-mani bangles, my husband's kaashi-taali chain,' she sighed. 'My grandmother's wankis—an armlet, my great-grandmother's kamar-patta, a gold belt,' her fingers gripped her forearm, then her waist, 'all 18- and 24-carat gold! An emerald set Mr Shenoy bought me when we were newly married, gold jewellery for our temple deity, my husband's watches,' she sat back, 'both he and Harsh have a liking for fancy watches. All gone! But as I told the police, I can put a price on all these items but the most precious of them,' she snivelled, 'it is priceless!'

Aaji edged closer.

'We lost our precious murti of Mahalsa Narayani...'

'That's your family deity?' inquired Aaji.

'Yes, our kula devi,' nodded Mrs Shenoy. 'It was a rare pancha-loha idol, nearly eight hundred years old. Our ancestors...' she pulled the pallu of her saree over her shoulder, 'they...they gave up their lives for it.'

Malhar looked at his sister quizzically. *Gave up their lives to save an idol?* Equally puzzled, Meera shrugged back.

'You see,' Mrs Shenoy launched into an explanation. 'When the Portuguese came to India four hundred years ago, they attacked many places in Goa, including my ancestral village in Konkan. Everywhere they went, they took forcible control of people's land, destroyed temples, smashed idols. When my forefathers got news that the Portuguese were advancing, they knew the fate that awaited them if they didn't resist. So they decided to fight.'

Meera had studied about Vasco da Gama's voyage to India and the arrival of the Portuguese as some watershed moment in the history of exploration and discovery. But she had no idea about this side of the story.

'Naturally, my ancestors were defeated as the firangis had better weapons but even as they lost and retreated, they tried saving the idols of the gods. They buried them in fields, dropped them into wells, in the hope that someone would retrieve them later. Many lost their lives in protecting these idols. Our Mahalsa Narayani—so big—' she said, holding out her palm, 'about 6 inches long, was found years later by my great-great-grandfather. Ever since, it has been with the eldest in the family and we honour it above everything. And I...'

she sobbed. 'Oh what face will I show my forefathers when I die?'

Aaji put a caring arm around Mrs Shenoy's shoulder. The old lady dabbed her eyes with the pallu of her saree.

'You know,' she continued. 'A year ago, one art historian,' she closed her eyes and tapped her forehead trying to recall. 'Some Abhay Mitra or something, a history or art professor—he visited us. Said he could get us a good deal for the idol from a museum where it would be displayed as national heritage. I refused outright. Told him it's my family heritage first! That I would give up my life but not the murti!' she continued sobbing. 'But look at this ugly twist of fate. Destiny wanted us separated.'

Meera exchanged glances with Malhar. This seemed much more complex than a simple case of robbery.

'I have failed to honour the blood and sacrifice of my forefathers,' wept Mrs Shenoy. 'My husband has been suffering from headaches and palpitations for the last three days. We will have no sleep till our Narayani is back.'

8

Arrested!

Whistling a merry tune, Mirchi sauntered past a yellow metal board with large red letters that read: 'Aslam Malik Kabadi-ki-dukaan', and dropped his gunny sack to the floor. His collection of paper, plastic, metal, and more, made its way here at the end of each day, where it was weighed, then sorted, before joining other materials in the long pipeline forming the enormous recycling industry of India.

At a table by the window sat a bespectacled middle-aged man with a screwdriver in hand, peering into a dismantled microwave oven. 'Koi lottery lagi hai aaj?' he chided Mirchi about his bright shirt.

'Kya, Aslam chacha,' Mirchi stopped whistling. 'Lottery-vottery is for chillar party,' he patted Javed, the lanky assistant boy bent over a pile of plastic bags on the floor. 'I dabble in the big game!'

Javed glared at Mirchi. 'Tu chillar party,' he grunted, picking up the sack and throwing it onto a weighing scale.

Ordinarily, Mirchi would have wasted no time in returning the rebuke. But today, little could dent his mood or derail his mission. 'Tell me, dost,' he placed a friendly arm on Javed's shoulder. 'You know this plumber called Velu?'

Javed fixed Mirchi with a glare, then flicked the boy's hand off his shoulder. Aslam chacha turned around to peer at Mirchi from under his glasses.

'It's nothing important,' fibbed Mirchi, to deflect unwanted attention. 'Some plumbing-vlumbing at home.'

'Plumber toh bahut mil jayenge,' said Aslam chacha, watching Javed weigh Mirchi's junk collection. 'Why do you want this Velu fellow?'

'Arre this Velu fellow fixed our tank last month and it's leaking already! My Dadi wants to give him a dose.'

'If he fixed your tank last month, you must know where he works,' shrugged Aslam Malik.

'Ah..haan...' Mirchi smiled, realizing his error. If he wanted to play this detective game, he'd have to be sharper. 'I forgot to ask Dadi where he works, and I don't want to go all the way back home to ask her. So I thought perhaps you might know.' He tried making amends. 'If you know, just tell me where I can find him.'

'Thane mein!' replied Javed.

'Hain?'

'PULIS TAY-SUN...' Javed explained through a mouth full of paan.

‘Police station?’ Mirchi narrowed his eyes.

‘The badmaash was arrested,’ said Aslam Malik. ‘Just on the day you have plumbing work. I wonder if there’s some connection,’ he smiled mischievously.

‘Arre...no, no! What connection can I have with him?’ Mirchi shrugged. ‘Kaunsa station?’

‘Why? You plan to complain there about your leaking tank?’ grinned Aslam Malik.

‘Kya firki letaa, chacha,’ Mirchi tried masking his curiosity with casual banter. ‘But what did this Velu do?’

‘Chori kiya,’ Javed’s eyes twinkled at the mention of his previous line of work, almost as if he missed those thrilling days. ‘At Customs Colony.’

‘Chori?’ Mirchi stuck out his tongue and held his ears, as if he was being told about some grave sin. ‘Baap re!’

‘Go check at Murugan Plumbing,’ Aslam Malik handed Mirchi a tenner for his scrap.

‘This Velu fellow works at Murugan Anna’s shop?’ asked Mirchi, pocketing the note and throwing his empty sack over his shoulder. ‘Phir toh no tension,’ he smiled. ‘I know Anna. Last year, when Dadi was in hospital he did blood donation, matching group tha uska.’

‘Good, then go ask someone there to fix your tank,’ said Aslam Malik, turning back to tackle the oven with a screwdriver. ‘And don’t get yourself into trouble!’

9

Usual Suspects

'Do you suspect anyone?' whispered Aaji, as the evening sun cast long shadows of the bakul trees at the edge of the temple complex, from which the town of Maulsari got its name. 'What about your maid? I hear she had your keys.'

Mrs Shenoy clicked her tongue. 'I trust her completely. So often I've misplaced a ring, a watch, or Mr Shenoy would drop some cash and Sarla has found them while cleaning the house and returned them. No!' she said with an emphatic shake of her head. 'Sarla could never have done it.'

'But why did you fire her then?'

'I have no doubt. But Harsh thinks after this episode, it would be foolish to continue with her. Mr Shenoy also agrees. So I'm left with no choice.'

'Anyone else had your house keys?'

'Mr Shenoy and I have one set each, one set is with my son Harsh who lives above us, our neighbours have one for emergency, and one was with Sarla,' she said. 'And none of those have been lost.'

'I heard from the watchmen that some plumber had come to your place around noon,' said Aaji, as Meera sat back, marvelling at her grandmother's interrogation skills.

'Yes, he was there for only five minutes to fix the washer in my kitchen sink. And I was standing right there beside him as he worked. Then walked him to the door. Na! It can't be him.'

'That young girl who lives with you,' enquired Aaji. 'She is...?'

'That's Preeti, my niece,' nodded Mrs Shenoy. 'She's from my native-place and is now studying here at National College. Since we're in Maulsari, I told her to stay with us. Why live alone in a hostel?'

A honk jolted them out of their conversation. They turned around to find a black SUV by the gate at the bottom of the temple steps.

'Ah, Harsh is here,' Mrs Shenoy propped herself up with her walking stick. 'After his office, he picks up Aditya from his chess classes, then comes to get me every evening on his way home. May God bless everybody with such a wonderful son.'

They turned around to find Harsh taking off his shoes at the bottom of the temple steps, then racing up with his young son Aditya. 'Namaste, aunty,' he smiled awkwardly, hands folded before Aaji, then bent down to touch her feet.

'Arre arre,' Aaji stepped back, taken by surprise.

'Dadi ko namasate karo,' Harsh nudged his little boy forward, beckoning him to do the same.

'May God bless you both,' Aaji placed her palm over their heads.

'Hello, champ!' Harsh ruffled Malhar's hair, then nodded at Meera. They returned his greetings with polite smiles, and waved to Aditya as the boy got a cuddle from his grandmother.

As they stood around, Meera couldn't help but notice that Gilderoy Lockhart did not look his usual self. The charming smile was missing, the cheerful demeanour was gone. Instead, he had dark baggy circles under his eyes, deep furrows creasing his forehead, a stubble on his chin. Clearly, it had been a stressful time for the family. And yet, like his mother, he too was elegantly dressed in a navy blue Hugo Boss shirt and black trousers, stylish Ray-ban sunglasses tucked over his head, and the whiff of an expensive musky perfume lingering about him.

'I'll be back in a minute,' said Harsh, rushing into the temple with Aditya. Meera and Malhar's eyes followed them, as father and son stopped to pray at every niche before every deity, Harsh patiently lifting his son to ring every bell, and fishing out coins from his pocket for the child to drop into every donation box.

'It is really wonderful to see how well your family has coped with this,' said Aaji to Mrs Shenoy, with an appreciative shake of her head. 'After all the strain you've been through.'

'Vidhi ka vidhan hai,' Mrs Shenoy pointed to the skies. 'Who can change the tide of destiny? In fact, just yesterday our society secretary Mr Shekhar asked us if they should go ahead with the Ram Navami celebrations of the colony next week. Every year, my bhajan group performs and Harsh and some others help the children put up a play. I told Shekhar the show must go on. It would not be right to stop it because of our personal problems.'

'With this positive nature, and the Lord's blessings, I am sure you will soon have your murti back,' Aaji reassured Mrs Shenoy, as her son and grandson returned.

'Aunty, shall I give you all a ride home?' asked Harsh.

'Uh...no...thank you,' Aaji smiled. 'We'll walk back.'

As Harsh pressed his palms together before Aaji to say goodbye, then held his mother's frail hands to lead her down the steps, Meera noticed the many rings with coloured stones on Harsh's fingers, a gold Rolex watch on his wrist, sparkling bangles on Mrs Shenoy's delicate hand, diamond earrings glittering on her ears. Clearly, everyone in this family had a love for expensive jewellery, she thought. And the thief, whoever it was, had had ample opportunity to make note.

'What a wonderful family,' Aaji exhaled hard, watching as Harsh held the car door open for his mother. 'Why must bad things happen to good people? The poor lady, she's wilted like a plant without sunlight. You children ought to learn from them. Look, how despite their troubles they are still so respectful and dignified. Malhar, especially you, weeping and whining at the slightest of problems!'

'Aaji! I am not like that anymore,' protested Malhar. 'But yes, when I grow up, I will be like Gilderoy Lockhart uncle. I'm going to have a big fancy car. And a watch like his Rolex.'

'Arre deva!' Aaji thwacked her forehead. 'I tell this boy to get me an apple, and he brings me a tomato!'

As they descended the temple steps to leave, Meera pulled out the blue diary from the bag, flipped open to the title page and scribbled a line under the first.

Mystery of the Stolen Jewellery

Mystery of the Missing Idol

Charged by Mrs Shenoy's story, touched by Harsh's caring nature, Meera felt more determined than ever to help, as she watched their black car pull out of the gate. Slowly but surely, they would chip away the layers, cut through the fog, and uncover the facts. Because sometimes, the truth lays concealed behind layers of deceit.

10

Search Operation

Mirchi turned into the long alley, his eyes instantly spotting the ruckus up ahead. 'What's that raada there?' he asked a woman pounding spices outside a masala shop on his left.

'Police,' she said, even as she continued her work.

Clambering on to a platform to get a better look, Mirchi noticed a crowd swelling outside a store with a board that read: MURUGAN PLUMBING WORKS. He hurried on, snaking his way through the onlookers towards the scene.

'Listen, Anna,' a beefy police officer with a big nose was yelling at Murugan Anna at the door of his shop, outside which lay a heap of materials. 'Tell me the truth, else you'll live to regret it.'

'I'm telling the truth, sahib,' Murugan Anna grovelled before the policeman. 'I don't know anything about this. Velu just went to repair something at that madam's house. We...we don't know anything.'

'You think I was born yesterday?' the inspector snarled, holding Murugan by his collar. 'I know how you operate. I'm sure you're involved. That boy Velu is your nephew, isn't he? The watchman at the colony says the plumber was the only outsider who entered the building that afternoon.'

Mirchi's eyes went to the name-badge on the man's uniform. 'Sa-an-j...j...j-ya Sh...Sh...ev—' he struggled to read the letters.

'And he sleeps in your shop, doesn't he?' the inspector shook Murugan. 'Where else will he hide the stolen maal? Aye Kadam, check properly!' he barked instructions to his deputy who was searching inside the shop.

Boxes filled with pipes and rings came flying out of the shop door in response to the inspector's orders.

'Velu has done nothing wrong, sahib,' Murugan pleaded with folded hands. 'I...we...it...' he stammered, too stunned to speak.

'First, learn to speak Hindi properly if you want to live in this country,' the policeman snapped. 'Else go back to your Madarasi hovel!'

'I...I was born here, sahib, this city is my home...'

'Zyada shaana mat ban!' the inspector twisted Murugan's arm. Then he turned to a tailor standing by a wooden stool in a narrow space outside the plumber's shop. 'And you!' he barked, pulling up the man, 'Sulaiman

Ladies Tailor,' he read the little board hanging on the sewing machine. 'Are you also involved?'

'No, sahib,' the tailor folded his hands. 'We are poor but honest people, sahib. We just do our dhanda and go home.'

'Which home? Bangladesh? Or Pakistan?' snickered the inspector, shaking the man violently like a rag doll. 'You act smart with me and I'll pack you rats off to where you belong,' he slapped him, swung him about and gave him a kick, sending the tailor flying towards the adjacent flour-mill, where he crashed into a stack of aluminium boxes. The inspector's belly shook with hysterical laughter as the tailor turned back spluttering, coughing, and caked with flour.

Mirchi clenched his teeth and tightened his fists, angered by the belligerence in the inspector's eyes, the arrogance in his voice, the smugness in his mannerisms. Having grown up in Anand Nagar, this was not the first time he'd witnessed this sort of scene. It was nearly a routine affair in this part of town. But each time, it gripped him with wild rage.

'One more day,' the inspector snapped his fingers, a demented grin fixed on his face, as his constables emerged empty-handed from the search inside. 'In one day if I don't have the maal, all you scoundrels will seriously wish you'd never been born.'

11

Fundamentals

'Yesterday this girl said she doesn't want to step into my office,' Madhavi Pradhan brought in a casserole from the kitchen and sat down at the dinner table. 'And today, she is drowning me in all sorts of legal questions. Earlier this evening, she was asking about the atrocities law. Then about my NGO client who works for the deaf and mute. Now she wants to know all about gathering evidence and conducting police investigations!'

'Meera, I am happy you are taking an interest in legal matters,' said the SSP, wiping his hands on a napkin and pulling up a chair. 'But first you need to understand the fundamentals. Then you can go into all these details.'

Malhar huffed as he stared at the steel plate before him. He wasn't looking for a lecture; only some basic answers.

'You need to understand that there is a basic difference between civil and criminal matters,' began their father as he served himself some salad.

'What does that mean?' Meera leaned forward, suddenly all ears.

'Alright,' the SSP rubbed his hands eagerly, 'let's say you have a watch. And Malhar takes it from you without your permission.' He winked at his son, knowing his fondness for watches. 'In other words, he steals it. Could you complain to the police for that?'

'Of course,' said Meera. 'If he took my things and refused to give it back—that's wrong!'

'Now, second situation. Let's say Malhar has a house in his name, and enters into an agreement with you to sell his house to you,' the SSP reached for the bowl of dal. 'You both sign the agreement, and you also make an advance payment. But after that, Malhar refuses to transfer possession of the house to you. Can you complain to the police?'

'Of course,' nodded Meera again, as she tore into a roti. 'If he took my money and refused to give me the house later—it's wrong!'

'A wrong has been committed in both cases, hasn't it?' said her father, squeezing some lime into his bowl. 'But in the first case, you can file a police complaint. In the second case, you can't.'

'Why?' asked Malhar, his indifference swept away by a burst of curiosity.

'Because,' their mother served them vegetables, glad they were too distracted to refuse the extra helping. 'In the second case, Malhar has wronged you by breaking the agreement he had with you.' She looked at her daughter. 'As it involves a dispute between two private individuals or citizens, it is called a civil matter. And you, Meera, can file a civil case in court against Malhar to recover your money or to get possession of the house. But there's no punishment you can seek from the police.'

'However, in the first case,' the SSP took over again, 'Malhar has committed theft, disrupting order in society. A thief is not a threat to you alone, but poses a threat to people at large. Hence, it is a criminal offence and if found guilty, the law will punish him.'

'But...but,' Meera's eyebrows narrowed, 'who decides what is which? And how is one to know?'

'For starters,' replied the SSP. 'It is a matter of principle. You need to ask yourself—is it a private wrong or a public wrong? But to answer your question specifically, in India we have what is called the Indian Penal Code, which contains a long list of wrongs, you know, like theft, burglary, murder, dacoity, so on and so forth. This law may change, but in principle, these are classified as criminal offences. Because it puts the public at risk.'

'For instance,' continued their mother, pouring herself a glass of water, 'the thief who has stolen the jewels from Mrs Shenoy's house, he—'

'It could be a SHE!' protested Malhar.

'Ho na!' Aaji bobbed her head from side to side as she peeled a pomegranate. 'Just yesterday on *Crime Watch*, they showed two women pulling off a big online scam... these days, nobody can be trusted.'

'Alright,' smiled Madhavi Pradhan, 'he or *she* may steal from others in the future. So it is not only the Shenoys who stand to lose by the thief being at large. But the public in general.'

'And so,' said SSP Pradhan, rising from the table with his plate. 'In the first case, the government takes on the responsibility to catch the thief as he or *she*,' he winked at Malhar, 'has wronged the public. So you can complain to the police, which is an arm of the government, and they will investigate the matter. Then if the police find enough reason to suspect Malhar, they will file a case in court against him for theft and the judge will ultimately decide if Malhar is guilty. And if he is, what punishment is to be given to him.'

'But in the second case,' continued Madhavi Pradhan, 'it is only a matter involving the two of you. You can file a case against Malhar in a civil court to recover your money or get the house transferred in your name. But the government or the police will not be involved.'

'So coming back to your original question now,' said the SSP as he rinsed his hands at the wash basin, 'in the case of the house, all you need to establish in court is that you had an agreement with him, and he broke the agreement. But in case of the theft, you will have to prove two things. One, that he stole your watch. And two, that he has a guilty mind.'

'In legal terms that is called "mens rea", explained their mother. 'Which means, a culpable or guilty mind. So in a criminal case, you need to show not just that Malhar took your watch, but that he did so deliberately and with the intention of stealing from you. Not by mistake or by accident. Because if he took your watch by mistake, he can't be punished for it.'

'But...but,' interjected Meera. 'How can I prove that he did it intentionally?'

'By showing some sort of motive,' replied her father, as he reached out for a bottle of mukhwas. 'Maybe Malhar has asked you for your watch in the past. And you refused. And he fought with you to get it. Maybe he has written in his diary that he has always wanted a watch like yours and feels sad that he can't afford or find it. These sorts of things can help you establish that he took it with the intent to steal.'

'See, in cases where there is no direct evidence like a witness, motive becomes important to nail the guilty person,' explained Madhavi Pradhan. 'If you'd paid attention during my client meetings at office, you could have learnt a thing or two about these things.'

Finishing up her meal hurriedly, Meera ran to her diary to make a note.

MOTIVE

She wrote down the word, then underlined it twice, glad to have learned about a crucial angle in criminal investigations. And as soon as she'd put the word down on paper, her eyes lit up with a brainwave.

12

Hard Truths

Clinging on to the banyan's dangling roots with her arms and legs, Meera tried swinging like Mirchi, only to discover that it was much harder than it seemed. Down below, Malhar was on his elbows and knees, placing twigs in the path of marching ants, thrilled to have the column meander around his obstructions.

'There they are,' Meera jumped down as she spotted Mirchi and Munna approach from the distance, abandoning her conquest of the banyan. Munna came bounding towards them, tail wagging, tongue dangling. Putting her arms around him, Meera rubbed his black fur, then tickled him on the underside of his neck.

'Grrr...' Munna growled in contentment, conveying his affection for her with a rub of his wet nose.

Pulling out a packet of biscuits, Malhar held them high up above Munna, making him chase and run behind him.

'We have a lot to tell you,' said Meera, as Mirchi got there at a snail's pace. 'Yesterday, we met Shenoy aunty at the temple and found out so much.' She flipped open her blue diary where she'd noted every detail, then launched into a narration.

Mirchi flopped down, then began plucking blades of grass, and tossing them this way and that, as he listened to Meera.

'What about you?' Meera wound up her update. 'Did you find anything?'

'Dadi says these chor-police games are not for poor boys like me,' complained Mirchi.

'What?' Malhar paused playing with Munna. 'You told your Dadi about our plan?'

'Was I not supposed to?' Mirchi stuck out his tongue.

'Didi!' Malhar hit his palm on his forehead, 'I told you not to involve him.'

'Wait,' Meera turned to Mirchi. 'Yesterday, you were so excited to be a detective and solve this mystery. You said you'd look for the plumber. What happened suddenly?'

'Arre kal, I go looking for that Velu plumber. So I returning home with only 30 rupees in pocket. My Dadi, she mad with me. She asking what I doing full day. So I telling. Then she becoming fultus angry, like Maa Kaali,' Mirchi mimicked his grandmother's expression. 'She saying to me, "Mirchi, all this time-pass for rich baccha-log." Children like me have to work to fill our stomachs.'

Meera looked down, not knowing what to say.

'Then she saying me, all you ameer log always doubting garib people like Sarla and Velu, never you will suspect your own people,' he frowned, remembering Murugan Anna's plight.

'No, that's not right. Wait!' Meera turned back to her diary. 'Look,' she flipped open to her list of suspects. 'Yesterday, I found out about this art historian who was interested in Mrs Shenoy's idol. I suddenly realized last night that he may have done it. So I added him to my list.'

Mirchi's eyes darted perfunctorily to the diary. 'My schoolteacher saying, for me, kaala akshar bhains barabar because I not knowing to read. So she saying black letters and black buffalo—same to same for me,' he translated for their benefit.

Malhar suppressed a giggle; Meera kept a straight face. 'Look,' she tapped on her diary. 'I'll read and explain.'

SUSPECTS	MOTIVE
1. Sarla (unlikely)	For money
2. Sarla's husband (to check)	For money
3. Plumber Velu (to check)	For money
4. Abhay Mitra (to check)	For the idol
5. Unknown person	??

Somewhat reassured that Meera was not like the ameer-log his grandmother kept cursing, Mirchi's eyes fell upon a tourist bus pulling up by the beach across the road. He stood up, threw his jhola over his shoulder and began to run.

'Where are you going?' Meera called after him as Munna bolted behind his master.

'Let him go,' Malhar clicked his tongue. 'It was a stupid idea to include him in the first place. There's no M4...we're just M2!'

'Wait,' Meera gripped Malhar by his arm as Mirchi crossed over to the beach. 'He said he spent all evening checking about Velu.'

'Ya...so?

'So...' Meera jumped up and broke into a sprint behind Mirchi. 'So he must know something!'

Left without a choice, Malhar ran behind his sister.

Crossing the road at the edge of the maidan, brother and sister ran over to the bus parked near the beach, then walked all around it. But Mirchi was nowhere to be seen.

'Where did he go?' Meera peeped into the bus through the windows.

'Good he's disappeared,' Malhar huffed, holding his sides. 'Just forget him.'

Suddenly Mirchi emerged from under the bus, two plastic bottles in hand. He stared at the siblings. 'Arre, what you wanting now?'

'You said,' Meera panted, 'you said you spent all evening searching for Velu. So did you find him?'

Picking up some glossy pamphlets flying about the wheel of the bus, Mirchi looked at Meera. 'You very shaani!' he smiled, then ambled over to a large bin and began rummaging about inside with a wooden stick. He extracted two plastic bottles, a cola can, some used straws, empty wafer-packets, and tossed them into his sack.

'What will you do with all this?' asked Meera, watching Mirchi work with swift efficiency.

'Sell to Aslam bhai,' Mirchi shrugged, spotting a street urchin who was eyeing the tourist bus from a distance. 'I need to empty this, before that lizard gets here.'

'There's some glass here,' Meera pointed to discarded beer bottles near her feet. 'Is it of any use?'

'Arre haan! Aslam bhai paying more money for glass.'

Meera picked up the bottles and handed them to a giggling Mirchi. 'What happened?'

'You picking kachra like me,' Mirchi laughed.

Shoulders slumped, Malhar let out a laboured sigh. He'd thought his sister would make for a good detective; and here she was, turning into a ragpicker.

'So how much will all this fetch you?' Meera ignored her brother's glares, as she watched Mirchi flatten out a crumpled aluminium foil he'd extracted from the bin.

Kneeling beside Munna, Malhar winced at the dried scabs of chutney lining the wrapper that may have once contained a sandwich. But Mirchi tossed away the flakes without a thought, then wadded out the foil neatly to add to his collection. 'Around 15 to 20 rupees,' he said, stomping off to a pile of garbage he'd spotted on the footpath.

'Then? After that, will you be free?' Meera followed him, picking up a Pepsi can and two paper cups along the way.

Mirchi shook his head. 'Then I go to Patrakar Bazaar area,' he said, dropping to his haunches beside a pile of trash, then poking about with his stick. 'There I getting lot of paper kachra.'

'Then,' Meera grimaced, wondering how Mirchi could sit beside such smelly filth. 'You'll be free after that?'

'Man! People throw all kinds of things,' Malhar winced at the sight of a soiled diaper.

'Then I going Dockyard Road,' Mirchi replied, as he pulled out a plastic bottle. 'I no going back home till I getting at least 200 rupees. Nahi toh Dadi shouting.'

'Don't touch that, Mirchi,' said Meera, spotting used batteries. 'I learnt in school that these leaking batteries are dangerous, and you don't have gloves.'

'Gloves?' Mirchi let out an incredulous chuckle. 'That's what this stick is for!' He tossed the batteries aside.

'So you will be doing this the whole day?' Meera gasped, spotting a used sanitary pad in the trash.

'Phir kya? Monday to Sunday, morning to night,' said Mirchi, using his stick to push away batteries, diapers and sanitary pads so he could reach the cardboard box underneath, 'Mirchi collecting kachra.'

As Mirchi rummaged through the garbage, Meera's eyes turned to Malhar. She exhaled hard, realizing that perhaps her brother was right, after all. Maybe she'd been foolish to even think of something as bizarre as the M4.

13

An Extraordinary Pact

'Wait,' Meera ran behind Mirchi towards the trash cans near the food stalls. 'I have an idea!'

One eye on the paper plates in the bin, another on the siblings, Mirchi smiled slightly. Seldom, if ever, did people pay attention to him; and the few occasions when they did, was only to drive him away because he was standing too close for their comfort. To have anyone other than Munna chase him, and ask for his help, made him feel special.

'You know,' Meera caught up, 'there is a big ground behind our school with an open shed. It is filled with all sorts of old things—unused cycles, cardboard cartons, tyres...'

His hands continuing with their swift operation, Mirchi tossed plastic spoons and forks into his bag.

'There's also broken furniture and blackboards. Every broken thing in school gets dumped there. What if I manage to get you some of that?'

'Didi,' Malhar protested. 'What's wrong with you?'

'We aren't doing anything wrong,' said Meera. 'Those cycles are old and rusted. Nobody wants them. They belong to students who've left school long ago. Actually, they belong to nobody. And honestly, the school will be grateful to us for clearing up that mess. So it's two birds, one stone. We help Mirchi and we help the school!'

Turning to Munna, Mirchi's eyes twinkled as his mind worked out how much every cycle and tyre would fetch him.

'Look, we'll get you some stuff from there everyday,' Meera promised Mirchi. 'Then will you want to be a part of M4?'

Mirchi nodded vigorously, a smile lighting up his eyes.

'Then take this,' Meera unzipped her bag and pulled out a packet. 'Here,' she handed Mirchi a round broach, then held out another before Malhar.

'You made badges?' Malhar grabbed the pin from his sister. It had four golden stars pasted above the letter M and the number 4 painted in gold. 'We have epaulets like the police!'

Pinning his badge upon his shirt, Mirchi ran his fingers over the stars. He'd never felt so important!

'And you are a part of the M4 too,' Meera tied a ribbon with an M4 logo around Munna's neck.

'Woof!' Munna responded with a nuzzle.

'So now will you tell us what Velu said? And check on Sarla's husband?' Meera opened her diary. 'By the way, what is his name?'

'Arre Sarla's husband is a bewda,' Mirchi brushed off the second suggestion. 'That useless fellow is always drunk and in some gutter. That yeda cannot pull off a—'

'But is it not possible,' argued Malhar, 'that he took the keys from Sarla without her knowing, and stole the jewels?'

'Hmm...' Mirchi nodded thoughtfully. 'Phir toh I knowing what he doing with stolen maal. My Dadi saying when a bewda wins lottery, you finding him drinking—at bar!'

'Your Dadi is one smart woman,' Meera adjusted the badge on her T-shirt. 'So then you should check him out, because when we met Shenoy aunty at the temple yesterday, she said she was sure it isn't the plumber Velu. She said she was in the kitchen with him when he was working and then walked with him to the door—'

'Pakka?' Mirchi's eyes grew large.

'Yes, that's what she said. Why?'

'Then we must do something!'

'About what?'

'The plumber!'

'Meaning?'

'The police arresting Velu yesterday,' said Mirchi, his fist tightening as he recalled Murugan Anna's desperate pleas before the heartless policeman. 'And they harassing all his relatives and friends.'

14

Summer Project

'Murli kaka, we need a favour,' said Meera, wistfully approaching the house orderly stationed outside their house. He was leaning on his motorbike, laughing hysterically over a video on his phone.

'Bolo beta, what Murli do phor you?' asked the rotund constable through a mouth of misshapen paan-stained teeth.

'The school has given us a summer project—to visit a police station and make a site report. Could you please take us to the Sikkachowki police station?'

'Arre Deva!' Constable Murli tapped his balding head and stuck out his tongue. 'Your Baba...say nothing!'

'We...uh...forgot to inform him,' said Malhar. 'It's just a few streets away, and besides, you'll be in time for the 4 o'clock batch of pakodas at the halwai store opposite the station.'

Constable Murli's eyes twinkled. 'O-K...No-problem!' he smiled. 'Uncle Murli take you. Gopi,' he called out to his junior. 'I taking babalog. You taking charge,' he said, kick-starting his bike and asking the children to hop on. 'The farsan shop near Sikkachowki police station, world-famous jalebi and bhajiya,' he chuckled, as he sped off.

As Constable Murli bantered away through his helmet-covered head, Malhar and Meera exchanged purposeful smiles behind him. If Meera had placed her bets correctly with their curious-cat Aaji at the temple yesterday, Malhar had got it right today with the simple pakoda-loving constable. It was surprising how easy it was to get one's way around people, once you knew them well enough.

15

Stalking

Satisfied with the day's earnings from a cycle, two switchboards and a tangle of wires that Meera had passed on from the school junkyard, Mirchi ensconced himself between two branches of a leafy palash tree that overlooked the alley leading to Sarla's house, crossed his hands behind his head, and closed his eyes.

At the foot of the tree, Munna was lying on his side, his black belly rising and falling as he waited in watch. After nearly an hour, his ears pricked up. 'Bhhow bhhow!' He stood up, stretched, and shook himself.

Mirchi awoke, noticed Sarla's husband Raghu stumbling out into the lane ahead, his feet unsteady, his gait awkward. 'Shabash, Munna,' he jumped down from the tree, threw his satchel over his shoulder and began following the man. Unlike most days, the fellow's shirt wasn't torn, his trousers weren't tattered, and he had slippers on. It raised Mirchi's antenna.

Winding through narrow lanes, Raghu reached the open space under a water tank where a pack of feral dogs were rummaging through a mountain of garbage. They barked at him, he hurled expletives in return, then trundled on, before turning towards an incline leading to a leather tannery.

Mirchi stayed at Raghu's tail, as the drunkard toddled alongside white animal hides strung across rows of bamboo poles for drying. Covering his nose to block out the overpowering stench, Mirchi slowed down, his eyes falling upon a workman astride a pit in the ground, swirling and rotating a large stretch of buffalo skin, then dipping it repeatedly into the alum inside. Distracted, he stopped to watch, his eyes drifting to another worker stomping a sheet of buffalo hide with his feet. 'Munna, how do these people use buffalo skin to make cricket balls?' He stopped and stared, overcome by curiosity, forgetting all about his snooping mission.

Startled by the entry of a spluttering tempo after a few minutes, Mirchi broke out of his stupor. 'Aila!' he hit his head, looking down the path Raghu had taken—neither Munna nor Raghu was visible. He ran along, looking this way and that. No luck!

'Tch,' Mirchi cursed himself for his sloppiness. 'Maybe all the teachers at school were right, Munna,' he scratched his head. 'Maybe I really am good for nothing!'

As if in answer to his innermost thoughts, Munna came running towards him, tugged him by the edge of his shorts and pulled him towards a broken wall.

'Ah! Shabash, Munna,' Mirchi patted the dog, and followed behind him, ducking through a hole in the middle of the wall to step onto the other side that led to an area filled with warehouses. Munna jumped out behind him.

Behind the wall, some workers from the tannery were bathing under a rubber water pipe, others changing out of their smelly work clothes under a babool tree. Following the dog, Mirchi walked past them, then past rows of warehouses, till Munna stopped and began to bark before a smallish structure.

'Desi daru,' Mirchi mumbled, hit by the smell of fermenting jaggery. 'Dekh Munna, Dadi was right,' he said, noticing bottles of country liquor strewn around.

Mirchi stepped closer to the building, pressing his ears to the walls. He could hear music inside, and suddenly someone began to yell.

Spotting a dusty window on the side, Mirchi ran towards it and peeped inside. He noticed the glint of glass bottles shining against the light, then the silhouette of some men playing cards on a table.

'Kya re!' one of them was pushing back another. 'Not a penny in your pocket and you want to live like a nawab?'

The other man said something inaudible, then pleaded before the first. Although the light inside was dim, Mirchi could tell the grovelling figure was Raghu.

'How dare you show up here?' the big fellow pushed him back again, as the others gathered around. 'First you pay back your udhaar!'

Again Raghu blabbered something incomprehensible to Mirchi.

'Pay back the money you owe me,' the man barked, pushing Raghu to the floor. 'And don't show me your face again till then. Now get out of here!'

'Yeda Raghu,' grunted Mirchi with a shake of his head, before turning around. Clearly, if the fellow was grovelling for small sums of money and getting beaten up for it, he had not committed a theft worth crores.

'See I was right, Munna,' smiled Mirchi, getting on for his evening round of junk collection. 'I am not so stupid after all.'

16

SHO

'O-k, we arriving,' announced Murli kaka, pulling into a compound at the centre of which stood a single-stored black-stone building. 'This,' he said, as he parked near a wall tumbling with pink bougainvillea, 'it was money-printing place in angrez zamana. What saying,' he snapped his fingers. 'Mint! Coin printing. So police station name is Sikkachowki,' he explained, placing his bike on the stand. 'Meera beta, you write that in project.'

Meera pulled out her diary, wishing she could turn in a project about this rundown police station, instead of some ancient stepwell which she had no interest in visiting. It was all about noting some architecture anyway. 'Shall we go inside?' she said, surveying the host of faces crowding the tin-roofed portico outside the building. At one end, someone was talking into a crackling walkie-talkie; at another, a woman seemed to be weeping about a missing child. Meera had not seen Velu, but had gotten a reasonable description from

Mirchi who had obtained the information from his sources. *Young boy, barely twenty. Very tall. Lean. Dark.* There were no matches.

'Look at all this,' Malhar grimaced, his eyes turned to bats hanging from the tall trees in the compound. He covered his nose and jumped over splotches of goo, as they walked past dozens of people milling about the portico and corridor.

'SSP sahib, bachalog,' Constable Murli announced with a self-important air, as they walked in, eliciting the immediate attention of all around.

Almost instantly, a bevy of men and women in uniforms stepped forward, nodding, smiling, shaking hands; some even made a casual salute.

Meera greeted them awkwardly, this being the very last thing she wanted. She hated it when people treated her differently because of her father's position, more so during a snooping visit like this, which she'd have preferred to keep quiet and discreet. Malhar, on the other hand, basked in the attention, quite pleased to march in like royalty.

'Arre arre!' a pot-bellied man with bushy eyebrows came rushing towards them. 'What an honour to have the children of the SSP sahib at my chowki,' he said, extending his stubby hand to greet them. 'Myself Sanjay Shevre. Inspector-in-charge of Sikkachowki thana. What can I get for you? Juice? Cold drink? Masala milk?'

'No no...nothing,' said Meera, noticing that the man's uniform was unlike her father's. The stars pinned to his shirt, the epaulets on his shoulder, the colour of the khakhi—everything was different. She remembered something she'd heard about how the IPS cadre, to which her father belonged, was different from the State Police from which police inspectors like Shevre were recruited, but she had no clear recollection. Suddenly she felt she ought to take more interest in getting to know the system.

'Please tell me how this humble Shevre can serve you?' asked the inspector, his eyes darting from Meera to Malhar and back to Meera, his head bent slightly in deference.

Accustomed to their Aaji's habit of denoting vegetables for people, Malhar couldn't help noticing the man's cauliflower-nose and large ears like onion rings.

Meera took a step back, a tad uncomfortable with the man's piercing gaze, her eyes on the golden filling twinkling in the inspector's mouth. He seemed to her like the kind of man who'd befriend people only to gain something in return.

'We...we have a summer project,' said Malhar. 'To visit a police station and write a report. So we asked Murli uncle to—'

'Good you chose to come here,' he said, giving his staff a knowing glare, as if to warn them to be at their best behaviour, lest a negative report reach the SSP's ears. 'Please feel free. Like your own home. You make report,' he said to them, beckoning a lady colleague. 'This is ASI Sakhi Pawar,' he introduced a diminutive sub-inspector. 'She will help you. Nandu,' he called out to someone else. 'Cold drink, biscuit lekar aa jaldi.'

Meera scribbled something into her diary.

'Ah! What are you noting down already?' The inspector pulled his leather belt over his oversized paunch, peeping into Meera's notebook.

'I had studied in school that child labour is an offence,' replied Meera stoically. 'So I noted down that a child is serving tea at the police station,' she pointed to the ganji-clad boy placing little glasses on the desks, 'and the policemen don't seem to mind.'

Inspector Shevre's face went red. With a signal of the eyes, he asked ASI Sakhi to take the children, before they could cause him further embarrassment.

Glad to have the sweet-talking inspector out of her way, Meera and Malhar followed ASI Sakhi, their eyes surveying the lock-up at the far end of the room. None of the five men inside matched the description of Velu. Malhar eyed a row of people seated on their haunches near the rear door with chains around their ankles. They didn't fit the bill either.

'Inspector Sanjay Shevre is the SHO of the police station, meaning Station House Officer, so he is in charge here,' ASI Sakhi began her tour earnestly. 'Under him, we are having four sub-inspectors...we say PSI, and eight assistant sub-inspectors, we say ASI. I am an ASI,' she pointed to the black badge on her uniform. 'And below us, there are constables—head constable, senior constable and junior constable. Of course, you must be knowing all this but...' she smiled.

'Oh no, please go on,' Meera nodded, grateful for the lesson, as they walked into a corridor.

'This is our store room,' Sakhi pointed to a door. They peeped in to find an assortment of things from hats to helmets and loudspeakers to lathis.

'Here we are having computer room,' Sakhi stopped at another door. 'We got our first computer last week,' she pointed to a monitor adorned with yellow marigold flowers. 'But we don't have Internet yet,' she added sheepishly.

As they walked past more corridors and rooms, Meera's eyes fell on a paper calendar under a glass-topped table with an image of Ganesha, and she was reminded of the purpose of her visit. *Idol. Theft. Velu.* 'Is there another lock-up inside?' she asked, pointing to the corridor that wound itself around the building.

'Yes,' nodded ASI Sakhi 'There is another lock-up at the back.'

'I...uh...want to go to the bathroom,' said Meera, without missing a beat, hoping to end the supervised tour.

'Actually,' ASI Sakhi winced. 'There is no ladies' bathroom in the police station. We have been asking since long time. Sorry, but you have to adjust.'

'Where's the boy's bathroom?' Malhar took the cue. 'I want to go too.'

'It's at the back. Come,' ASI Sakhi began to lead the way.

'I am sure you have important work to do,' said Meera, 'I'll take him, and besides, Uncle Murli is with us,' she pointed to their house orderly who was fanning himself with a newspaper on a bench. 'We'll take a quick look and leave. Please don't take any more trouble.'

'As you wish.' The policewoman's head bobbed from side to side. Then after exchanging some thank yous and other pleasantries, much to Meera's relief, they were finally left alone.

17

Horror-struck

Turning the corner, Meera and Malhar scampered along the side of the stone building, past a water-cooler and a rumbling generator. Making yet another right turn, they emerged onto the rear side. 'Do you hear that?' Meera paused at the start of the dimly-lit corridor.

'What?'

'Someone is crying...'

Inching ahead on their toes, they heard voices. The sobbing turned into howling, till suddenly the outline of two men appeared underneath a flickering tube light at the end of the corridor.

Meera pulled Malhar behind a wrought-iron spiral stairway, and they settled underneath its shadow.

As their eyes adjusted slowly to the dim light, the silhouettes became clear figures. Up ahead, was a small room with metal bars, presumably the other lock-up. On the inside was a young boy crouched over, weeping, grovelling. On the outside were two men standing, listening, nodding.

'Mama, kaapatu mama,' cried the boy inside, clutching the feet of the man outside through the metal bars. He said something through painful yelps. But neither Meera nor Malhar could follow a word.

'I think that's Velu inside,' whispered Malhar, as Meera's eyes filled with tears at every anguished howl escaping the boy's lips. 'And that must be his uncle Murugan. Looks like they're talking in Tamil.'

Peeping through the side of the stairway, Meera tried to focus her eyes on the sallow figure lit eerily under the flickering light. The figure matched the description of Velu alright, but his face was swollen, his left eye a bloody blob, and his bare torso covered with welts.

'They whipped him with belts,' Murugan translated Velu's words for his companion. Fortunately for the children, the other visitor appeared not to know Tamil. 'And tied him to that bar up there.'

Malhar stood frozen. Meera swallowed hard. 'But why did he run away?' asked the other man. 'Now they have more reason to suspect him.'

'He...he got scared!' Murugan translated Velu's reply. 'He didn't know what to do. The moment he heard there was a theft in the house he had just visited, and that the police were looking for him—he panicked. His mind didn't work.'

'But the police interpret that as guilt,' said the other man. 'And they're also saying he has a motive. That he stole the jewels to pay for his sister's wedding.'

'The wedding has been called off now,' Murugan shook his head despondently. 'The boy's father heard about the police case and broke off the engagement saying it will bring disrepute to his family.'

Velu said something again through more crying and howling.

'They thrashed him. Told him to admit to the crime. But how can he admit to something he never did?' Murugan continued with his translation, then pleaded for his friend's help. 'Raja, please arrange a lawyer soon. At this rate, they'll extract a confession by torturing him or beat our Velu to death.'

'This is precisely why a confession made before the police is not acceptable in court,' the other man was about to explain something when hurried footsteps in the corridor made them turn. 'Time up,' a constable strode up to the lock-up, then clicked his lathi on the metal bar.

The two visitors folded their hands before the constable. 'Please sahib, he is innocent, he's a young boy. Please don't beat him—'

'Chalo chalo,' the constable shepherded them away.

Assuring Velu that they would return soon, the two men retreated down the corridor, then disappeared around the bend.

'THWACK!'

A jolting sound made the children jump and turn around.

'Kya re?' the khaki-clad constable was inside the cell, striking Velu with his lathi. 'Complain karega?'

THWACK!

Another blow and slap, and Velu, weeping and whimpering, was flat on the floor.

Meera pressed her eyes shut and covered her ears, unable to bear the agonizing howls. *Was this the district police force her father presided over*? A chill ran down her spine.

Malhar shielded his eyes with his palms, then watched horror-stricken through the gap between his fingers.

'Tell us where you've hidden the maal by the end of the day,' yelled the constable. 'Else, this was just a trailer. I'll come back to add the finishing touches!' he warned, then stepped out of the cell, clicked the key into the lock, and marched off.

Peeping out from their hiding spot under the stairway, Meera caught sight of Velu, and let out a gasp. It was a nauseating sight, made ghostlier by the flickering tube light.

'When I grow up,' said Malhar, his lips quivering, 'I'm going to punch that policeman to pulp!'

Holding her brother's hand, Meera slipped out from behind the stairway. 'We have to find the thief soon,' she said gloomily, grateful to be out in the sunlit courtyard. This was no longer a summer adventure to fill their time. Nor a project to recover lost ancestral heritage.

It was now a mission to help Sarla and Velu, who were suffering for no reason at all. This was no more a simple case of burglary. Their task had acquired a deeper meaning; their effort, an urgent purpose. There was no turning back.

18

A Dark Encounter

'Teen tigda, kaam bigda!' Aaji laid out a set of three threes and other combinations of cards on the low table, underneath the glow of the emergency lamp. The lights were out in Maulsari on the warm summer evening, as they so often are in small towns across India, and they'd gathered in the veranda, the coolest place in the house for a game of rummy.

'Tch!' Malhar slapped a mosquito on his arm. 'How can you win again? I think you're cheating, Aaji.'

'Arre wah re bhoplya! If you win it's winning, if we win, it's cheating?' Aaji collected the cards and held them before Meera.

'Stop calling me a pumpkin na, Aaji!' protested Malhar, even as Meera stared at the rim of the table.

'Agga...ghe!' Aaji held out Meera's palm and deposited the cards into it. 'This girl is always lost in her own world.'

'Ma,' Meera began shuffling. 'Isn't a person supposed to be innocent until proven guilty? That's what I've heard in the movies. Even Dumbledore says it in *Harry Potter*.'

'Yes, that is mostly the case.' Madhavi Pradhan cocked her head, surprised by Meera's continued interest in legal matters. 'By the way, I told my NGO client about Sarla's daughter. They said they'll check about providing the child with a hearing aid. I'll give you their phone number. You can follow up.'

'What do you mean that is mostly the case?' Meera shot off another question.

'Usually....actually, almost always,' her mother began dealing the cards Meera handed her, 'the law assumes one is innocent until proven guilty in court. But in rare cases, like dowry death or domestic violence, or offences against children, the burden of proof may stand reversed.'

'As in?' Meera barely looked at the cards in her hand, even as the others arranged theirs.

'As in, if I accuse you of stealing my phone, I have to prove that you have stolen my phone,' explained Madhavi Pradhan. 'On the other hand, if a newly married girl dies within a few months of her wedding, and her parents allege that the death has been caused because of dowry pressures, it is the bride's husband and in-laws who will have to prove that the death was not a dowry death. The burden of proof shifts to the other side because of the skewed power equations and the large number of such cases.'

'But if you haven't proved that I stole your phone,' Meera stayed focused on theft, 'can the police put me in the lock-up and beat me up?'

'Chalo! Get ready for one more lawyer in the family,' grunted Aaji, tapping Meera on her shoulder. 'It's your turn, play now!'

'Of course not!' replied her mother. 'Firstly, in technical terms, I don't have to prove anything. It is the police who have to investigate. Remember, I told you that in a criminal offence, the police takes charge?' She paused, picked up a card from the common pile, examined it and put it back down.

'Ma, then what?' asked Meera impatiently, as an owlet hooted from the tamarind tree and cicadas croaked in the distance.

'So during the investigation,' continued Madhavi Pradhan, 'if the police find reason to believe that you stole it, they'll file what is called a chargesheet in court against you. Then the judge will hear the case where the police's lawyer, known as the prosecutor, will try and prove that you are the thief and then...' she paused, distracted by the cards in hand.

Meera shook her mother's arm. 'Then what?'

'Uh...then,' Mrs Pradhan played her card, then continued, 'you can argue that you did not steal it and try to disprove the police's case. Finally, after hearing all sides, the judge will decide. And then if you're found to be guilty, you will be put in jail.'

Meera was puzzled. 'But...but...then how--'

Her words were swallowed by the roar of an engine, then the beam of approaching headlights drowned them all in its bright glow. Another car rolled in behind the first.

'Not bad, back before midnight today,' Madhavi Pradhan checked her watch, then held her hand up to block the glare as they heard footsteps and chattering voices.

The headlights died out, as SSP Pradhan and another figure strode up the three steps and into the tiled veranda. Jumping up, Malhar ran to his father, Meera kept her eyes on the big man by her father's side.

'Everyone, meet Samir, my batchmate from the academy,' Baba introduced the oval-faced man. 'Aai, you remember Samir Naik?'

Aaji stood up and adjusted her glasses.

'Remember I had this batchmate who was a huge Rajni fan?' smiled SSP Pradhan, mimicking the trademark Rajnikanth move of tossing a cigarette up into the air and into his mouth. 'We used to call him Pasha,' he laughed. 'I just happened to run into him. What a coincidence! It's been years since we met.'

Aaji nodded, a faint hint of recognition in her eyes.

'Namaste, Maji,' Officer Naik pressed his palms together.

Aaji's lips curved into a slight smile, she remembered the fellow as *brinjal-face*. 'So are you posted in Maulsari too?'

'Arre no,' SSP Pradhan patted his friend. 'He's now Deputy Commissioner Economic Offences, posted at the capital,' he smiled. 'Big man!'

'C'mon!' Mr Naik played it down. 'I'm one amongst many fish in a big city. But you, my friend,' he threw an arm around SSP Pradhan, 'are the boss of the district!'

'Please come in,' said Madhavi Pradhan.

'Oh no, I've got to go. Actually, I had no idea Danny had been transferred here,' he said. 'Else I'd have kept aside some time to meet up. But when we bumped into each other, I thought I'd just pop in to say a quick hello. I'm only here for a few days to visit my wife's side of the family. They'll be waiting for dinner. I should go. Very pleased to meet you all.' He patted Malhar and Meera, folded his hands together before their mother and grandmother, then gave his friend a hug before turning to leave.

'Next time you're here,' SSP Pradhan accompanied his friend to his car, followed by Meera and Malhar, 'let me know beforehand.'

'Definitely boss,' Samir Naik shook hands with him, then got into his car, closed the door and lowered his window. 'Hopefully in better weather,' he winked, as he dabbed his sweaty forehead thrice with a handkerchief, before his car sped off.

'Baba, you're late again!' complained Malhar, as they turned back to the house. 'You said you'll come early and play badminton with us today!'

'Sorry...sorry,' the SSP trudged back. 'I got busy with some meetings. But how about some chess instead?'

'Arre let Baba eat first.' Aaji gathered the playing-cards into a box as Madhavi Pradhan hurried off to lay the dinner table and the SSP went in to shower.

Back in the living room, as Malhar laid out pieces on the chess-board, Meera sunk back into the couch, troubled by unanswered questions.

What she had seen today just didn't add up with what her mother had explained.

Where and when had the police proved that Velu was the thief? And if they hadn't, why on earth was the poor fellow behind bars?

19

Ally

'What were you doing at the police station yesterday?' asked Mrs Ghosh, without looking up from the brightly coloured canvas on the table.

Meera's mouth fell open. Malhar stared at his art teacher.

'I was at Mohan Halwai,' said Paromita Ghosh, their art teacher, matter-of-factly. 'Opposite Sikkachowki. I was surprised to see you inside.'

'We...uh...'

'Ahhhhha!' Mrs Ghosh flashed a knowing smile. 'If I had any doubts, they've vanished now. Your faces make it clear you were up to something! So, tell me, tell me,' she winked, adding a touch of white to lighten the sky Meera had painted.

'Actually...we,' Meera exchanged glances with Malhar.

'You see, if it's something to do with the theft at the Shenoy's house,' said Mrs Ghosh wiping her paint-smeared fingers with a cloth, 'I am both curious and concerned. After all I live in the same building. And besides, I am a big fan of Byomkeshda. Not having an answer to a mystery literally right under my nose makes me very restless.'

'Bomkeshda?' Malhar's eyebrows furrowed.

'Eh! Not Bomkesh,' Mrs Ghosh looked up from under her black-rimmed glasses. 'Byomkesh Bakshi. Have you not heard of him?'

The children shook their heads, prompting Mrs Ghosh to push back her chair and walk over to a large bookshelf in the living room. 'Here,' she said, dusting some books with the pallu of her sari before placing it on the table strewn with art materials. 'The children of today!' she sat back with a sigh. 'They know Nancy Drew and Hardy Boys but not Byomkesh Bakshi!'

'But Aunty these books are in Bengali,' Meera examined the collection.

'Ehhh...that is so,' said Mrs Ghosh, flipping a book open. 'You see, Byomkesh Bakshi calls himself satyavenshi—meaning truth-seeker. His only interest is to find the truth. When I was growing up in Siliguri, I wanted to be like him, and my brother, my neighbour and I would try solving all kinds of local mysteries in our tea estate, pretending to be Byomkeshda!' she laughed, finishing her touch-up on Meera's oil landscape. 'This one time, we helped find the man who'd stolen our teacher's chain. Another time, we tracked down a worker pinching money from the petty-cash box at the estate manager's office. It was so thrilling.'

Meera looked at the painting, then at their art teacher. Clearly, they weren't alone in their quest to solve mysteries; generations before them had been there and done that. Malhar reached out for a piece of sandesh on the table even as he exchanged more telling glances with his sister, both gradually warming up to the idea of turning their teacher into a confidante.

'I sometimes wonder,' said Mrs Ghosh, dropping her voice to a suspicious whisper, 'if that girl Preeti who lives with them is somehow involved...'

'Really?' Malhar's eyes grew large; the thought never having crossed his mind. 'You think she can steal from her own aunt and uncle?'

'If I've learnt one thing in all my years of reading crime,' said Mrs Ghosh, 'it is that you must never rule out those that seem unlikely. The more unlikely the suspect, the more you ought to suspect them.'

'Hmmm...' Meera nodded, convinced Mrs Ghosh would make an excellent ally in their operation. 'Aunty, we went to the police station to get information about the burglary,' she confessed. 'And like you, we also have a partner with whom we are trying to solve the case. And honestly, it never struck us that this Preeti could be a suspect. Maybe we should check if she's got a motive,' she said, recounting the new concept she'd learned about.

Mrs Ghosh absentmindedly scribbled M-O-T-I-V-E with a pencil on the edge of a folded newspaper. 'You see motive,' she said pensively, 'is only one part of the equation. The other part—perhaps more important—is means.'

'Means...' repeated Malhar. 'Means?'

'Means as in access...opportunity...chance. Many people may have a motive to steal. Anybody who wants to get rich quickly, or has some money trouble like their maid Sarla. But the question is—did they have the chance?'

Meera nodded thoughtfully, then leaned into her bag and pulled out her blue diary. Opening to her notes, she added a word under MOTIVE.

MEANS

Then she underlined it twice.

Flipping pages, she turned to her list of suspects and added a name.

5. Preeti Shenoy (Mrs Shenoy's niece)

'Who is this plumber Velu?' asked Mrs Ghosh, peering into the list in the diary.

'A plumber who went to repair something in their kitchen that afternoon,' replied Malhar.

'But the plumber most certainly didn't do it!' Mrs Ghosh looked surprised.

'That's what it seems...but how do you know?'

'Because, just as the boy was coming out of Shenoy's house that afternoon, I was in the lift coming home. I saw him and requested him to come to my house to take a look at my leaking washbasin. He came immediately and had only a small plastic bag with some tools. He fixed the problem, then went straight out. From my window, I saw him walk out of the building.'

'But...but why haven't you told the police?' asked Meera. 'They're beating the poor guy black and blue!'

'O bhogoban!' cried Mrs Ghosh. 'I had no idea! I'll go and tell the police,' she said, glad to have a chance to get involved in the investigation. 'And you two, I say you keep an eye on that girl Preeti,' she said, helping the children gather up their art-work. 'If Byomkeshda were here, he'd have said everyone has a weakness, look out for it. Eventually, the culprit is bound to make a mistake and reveal their weakness. Just wait for that moment. All these years reading Byomkesh Bakshi...' she said, dropping her voice to a whisper again, 'tell me that it's an inside job!'

20
Alibi

'Alibi!' Meera exclaimed, swinging from a woody liana in a thicket at the back of Customs Colony, as they watched a group of workmen putting up bamboo poles and a bright red shamiana for the Ram Navami festivities that were to take place a few days later. 'We should check the suspects' alibis.'

'Alibi matlab?' Mirchi jumped down from his perch on the karanj tree.

'Means, we check where the suspects were at the time of the robbery. Let's start with suspect number 1,' Meera flipped open her diary. 'Where was Sarla on the afternoon of the robbery?'

'Sarla saying she in her house,' replied Mirchi. 'Chilbil also telling me her mother finishing morning kaam, then taking her from school, then going home.'

Meera nodded, holding out a box with slices of watermelon. 'Can you confirm?'

Mirchi looked at the fruit hesitantly, unsure if he could touch it.

'Take.' Meera thrust the box forward. 'Next on our list is her husband.'

'Arre that fellow is a waste.' Mirchi took a piece, as he examined the canopy of the mango tree above them. 'He having no bheja to plan chori!'

'And Didi, would a fellow who's stolen so much money be begging his friends for money?' Malhar reminded her of Mirchi's findings, holding a biscuit before Munna. 'Let's not waste our time with him.'

Meera tapped the diary with her pencil. 'Then we have the plumber Velu.'

'I think we should cancel him out,' said Malhar, 'after what Ghosh aunty told us.'

'But we should check where he was that afternoon after leaving Customs Colony,' said Meera. 'It will help his case.'

'I checking,' Mirchi spit out watermelon seeds into the thicket and reached out for another slice in the box, this time with some confidence.

'Next on our list is Abhay Mitra,' Meera tapped the diary with her pencil. 'The art historian.'

'I know he may have a motive,' Malhar rubbed Munna's belly. 'But how on earth would he get into the house? He didn't have the means!' he said, throwing around the newly learnt idea. 'The person who actually had the MEANS,' he said, 'is Suspect Number 5—Preeti!'

'Good point.' Meera munched on the juicy watermelon. 'We should find out where she was that afternoon.'

'Mrs Shenoy told us she was at college,' said Malhar, watching Mirchi swing onto the mango tree and casually clambering further up.

'That's what Mrs Shenoy assumes,' shrugged Meera, putting away the empty fruit box. 'We should confirm that.'

'See,' said Mirchi, seated on his haunches on a broad branch of the mango tree, 'one way to hold your nose is this,' he tapped his nose with his right hand. 'The other...is like this...' he twisted his right arm around his head to reach for his nose from the left side.

Meera stared at him quizzically, as Malhar got busy trying to mimic Mirchi's effort to scale up the tree.

'My dadi saying—jab seedhi ungli se ghee na nikle, ungli tedhi karni chahiye,' Mirchi explained. 'First we try solving case by looking for chor. But there is one more way.'

'And what is that?' Meera stood below the mango tree, hands on her hips.

'By looking for the stolen things!'

'But how do we do that?' Malhar dangled from a low branch, then dropped to the ground.

'Can you get me some fancy girly items?' asked Mirchi, his eyes searching for ripe mangoes.

'What?' Meera's eyebrows furrowed.

'You know, earrings-sheering, chain-vain. Young girls liking...' Mirchi plucked two mangoes, tucked it into his shirt and climbed higher looking for more.

'What do you need all that for?' Meera called out, craning her neck to spot Mirchi.

'For Fawda,' said Mirchi from somewhere inside the tree.

'Who?' Meera shouted, barely able to see the boy in the dense canopy.

'Fawda!' repeated Mirchi, sliding down a portion of the tree-trunk, then landing with a thud.

'You know someone named Fawda?' snickered Malhar. 'As in like...SPADE?'

'Arre his asli name is Javed but he has buck teeth,' Mirchi stuck his front teeth out of his mouth to explain, 'so everyone calling him Fawda. See, there are five Javeds in Anand Nagar so mechanic is Javed-scooter, paan-wala is Javed-beedi, handsome one is Javed-chikna—'

'Okay, okay,' Malhar stopped him. 'So what about this Fawda fellow?'

'He working in Aslam Chacha's bhangaar shop now. But till two years back, he being chor—you know, chain-snatcher?' Mirchi wiped the mangoes with the edge of his shirt then handed one each to Meera and Malhar and bit into the third. 'I sure he knowing places where chor-log taking stolen maal for selling. So I asking him. But he not telling.'

Meera nodded, noting that Mirchi had handed them the riper of the mangoes and kept the raw one for himself. 'Hmm...so maybe he can give us some useful leads,' she said, touched by Mirchi's way of saying thanks for the watermelon. 'But...uh...why do you need girly gifts?'

'Fawda no give information for free, na?' explained Mirchi, his face contorting as the sour mango tickled his tongue. 'Why he give? But he liking one girl,' he said with a sly smile. 'Her name Rasheeda. Now if I giving him some fancy-vancy gift item to give her, he become happy and ready to tell me.'

'What logic!' Malhar grunted, as displeased with the mango, as with Mirchi's idea.

'Wait. Ma gets all these fancy gifts from her clients that she never uses,' said Meera.

'Didi! You can't just take Ma's stuff and give it to some...some Fawda person,' winced Malhar.

'Perfume bottle,' Meera's eyes lit up with an idea. 'Ma gets a few each year as gifts and she hates them... she's allergic to perfumes. So she's stored them all away and told me I can use them when I grow up. So technically,' she gave Malhar a no-nonsense purse-of-lips. 'Technically, they are mine. I can do as I please with them.'

Malhar looked up from the mango in his hand and glared at Mirchi. First the boy had taken a shirt from him, then a cricket bat. He had an eye on his Spider-

Man watch, and now some fancy perfume. He didn't like this trend.

'You knowing, police having khabri-vabri,' said Mirchi. 'Mukhbirs or informants like auto-rickshaw-wala, paan-wala, to get information about criminals. They giving them paisa for chai-vaai, to keep them happy. If we want to play chor-police,' he winked, tossing the mango seed into the thicket, 'we also needing some khabris like Fawda.'

Crossing her hands before her, Meera nodded, then shot Malhar a telling smile. This was precisely why they needed a partner like Mirchi. Birds of a feather flocking together can only get that far. To fly above and go beyond, they needed help—from the sun, from the wind, from the elements. Nobody gets anywhere alone.

21

Detectives in Disguise

A theft in a plush society like Customs Colony that housed top government officials was no laughing matter. That thieves had become so emboldened, to strike this close to the house of the Senior Superintendent of the District Police, only made it more alarming. Thus began the discussion between residents gathered around a clump of neem trees in the middle of the complex, after their morning walk, concerned about the pressing matter of strengthening security arrangements.

'Put the Ram Navami celebrations on hold,' an aged man tapped his walking stick, pointing agitatedly to the bamboo poles and ropes strewn about the makeshift stage. 'This is more urgent.'

'Please let us not mix up issues,' intervened Arun Shekhar, the mild-mannered society secretary. 'They are two separate matters.'

'We need an extra night watchman,' suggested someone.

'A burglar alarm system,' said someone else.

'ID cards for all the house-help,' said another.

'Bye Masi, I'm off to college!' Preeti waved to her aunt seated on a bench under a neem tree, walking through swirls of dust thrown up by the sweeper's broomstick.

'Eaten your nashta, beta?' called out Mrs Shenoy.

Dressed in blue jeans and an orange kurti, a green rucksack on her shoulder, Preeti held up her thumb, waved again, then rushed out of the gate.

Meera and Malhar emerged from behind the mango tree where they were lying in wait, pretending to be plucking low-hanging fruits. Then, skirting their way through joggers with headphones and seniors with walking sticks, they followed Preeti.

Partially covering her face with a brown dupatta, Meera adjusted her mother's large sunglasses over her eyes and peered at her reflection in the window of a parked car. *Good enough* she thought to herself, as she hurried behind Preeti towards the bus stop across the road.

Not one to be satisfied with a cover as dull, Malhar had decided this was his chance to pay homage to Fatty, who glided effortlessly into an array of disguises from balloon-seller to courier-boy. Retrieving his old shirt that Aaji had set aside to convert into a dusting cloth, and getting Mirchi to part with torn slippers from his scrap collection, Malhar had settled upon playing a beggar boy; then spent hours practising and polishing his act. He'd even added finer touches by smearing his face with grease, and digging his fingernails into potted plants to get them dirty.

Oblivious to being followed by face-covered girl and disguised beggar-boy, Preeti pulled out her phone, tucked earphones into her ears, and tapped some keys on her mobile as she waited at the bus stop. In a minute, Bus No. 21 pulled up and she prepared to board.

Getting into the queue, Meera and Malhar entered the bus behind her. Noticing their target make her way to the front, they followed. Preeti sat on the third row to the left. Spotting an empty space behind her, Meera slid onto the green rexine. Hobbling on, Malhar took pleasure at every stare he received from co-passengers, taking it as a tap on his shoulder for his superb disguise! He then took a seat across the aisle on the same row as his sister.

The bus got moving. Preeti got on a call and began whispering into her phone. Meera leaned forward, pretending to rest her head on the handlebar before her. She noticed Preeti's dangling earrings, a thin gold chain on her neck. But she couldn't hear much of the conversation except stray words. Quickly pulling out her diary, she began making note of them.

'Not now, money.' She heard the words loud and clear.

'Bad time...' That was another phrase she caught clearly.

‘Ticket ticket.’ The conductor came by, clicking his ticket meter. Preeti flashed a laminated card at him—a daily bus pass. Meera dug into her pocket to pull out a note. ‘National College,’ she whispered. ‘Same.’ Malhar handed a bunch of coins.

‘Papa…angry…’ Meera caught two more words. She noted them down.

‘I told you not now!’ more emphatic words, as the bus turned away from Dhyan Chand Maidan and the beach towards the interior of the city

‘Money… Job.’ Meera kept making notes. Perhaps later they could string these words together to make sense of them.

‘National College,’ the conductor tugged at the bell.

Malhar and Meera stood up, expecting to follow Preeti out of the door. But Preeti did not budge. Meera looked at her brother and shook her head, as they sat back down, even as Preeti continued yapping on her phone, throwing her head back to laugh every once in a while.

As the bus pulled out and the gates of National College whizzed past their window, Malhar exchanged glances with his sister.

Preeti had told her aunt she was going to college. Where was she really going? And why had she lied?

22

Khabri

'Yeh dekh, phoren scent.' Mirchi held the silver cardboard box before Javed, after checking to see that Aslam chacha wasn't around.

Javed's eyes lifted from the netted-sack he was filling with aluminium tins, then settled on Mirchi at the door.

'For ladies,' added Mirchi, with a twitch of his eyebrows.

The sack flopped onto the floor with a clang. Javed stepped towards Mirchi.

Mirchi opened the box and delicately prised out the crystal bottle. Then he twisted open its rose-petal-shaped lid and closed his eyes as he inhaled the fragrance.

'Full hai?' Javed's jaw dropped. 'Kidhar mila?'

'Rasheeda will like it very much.' Mirchi winked, placing the bottle on the wooden plank before him. Javed's eyes darted this side and that, then his fingers inched towards the bottle on the counter.

'You can have it.' Mirchi put the bottle back into his bag. 'But first you tell me.'

'Kya?' Javed's eyebrows knotted.

'Arre, I asked you that day na. Where chor-vor taking chori-ka-maal for selling,' Mirchi reminded him.

Javed stared at Mirchi. 'Bas? That's it? If I tell you, you'll give me the bottle?' It was to him the most elementary of questions. Like asking Tendulkar how to hold a bat—there just wasn't much to it.

Feeling like a policeman cultivating an informant, Mirchi grinned. From the corner of his eye, he spotted Aslam chacha returning from the public toilet at the end of the street, supported by a wooden crutch tucked under his left arm.

'Dekh,' Mirchi whispered. 'Tell me where chor-log selling jewellery. And yeh bottle tera!'

'Lunch time,' Javed lost no time to reply, before his uncle trundled back. 'Come to the adda below the tanki.'

23

Tour around Town

'Central Station,' announced the conductor, as the bus spluttered along a busy road leading to the city's main railway station. Then Patrakar Bazaar, followed by Sessions Court.

Preeti stayed put.

'Dockyard...Dockyard.' The conductor tugged at the bell as they passed a bridge overlooking large warehouses that formed the hub of the large Maulsari Port. Then Phool Galli, followed by Guntur Market.

Preeti hung up her call, then began checking something on her phone. But she did not get up.

Snivelling and sniffing, Malhar was enjoying the ride, content to observe the changing city and its smells as the bus wound its way through Maulsari—first the sea and fish, then flowers and spices. He was itching to share his astute observations with his sister, to tell her what a fine detective he'd make, picking up subtle signs most others would miss. But Meera had her anxious eyes pinned to the window.

'MG Road...MG Road.'

Preeti did not budge. Instead she turned on the front camera of her phone and started applying lipstick!

Meera began biting her nails. They did not know this part of the city. How much longer was this bus ride going to be? Wiping her sweaty face with her dupatta, she looked at the conductor handing tickets at the back of the bus. Would he give them another ticket now? But...to where?

'Hey!' a voice jolted her out of her worries. 'Don't you live in Customs Colony?'

Meera froze. With the dupatta and sunglasses off, her cover was blown! Preeti had seen her in the phone camera.

'Uh, yes,' Meera said in a meek voice, putting the sunglasses back on.

'Where are you going?' Preeti turned back to pout into the mirror.

'I...uh...'

'Majestic,' announced the conductor, the bell tingling again as the bus slowed down near a huge mall.

'That's my stop!' Preeti put back the lipstick and zipped her bag close.

Meera's face flushed with relief even as Malhar's had an all-knowing grin. Detectives did not lower their guard. She may not have learned that from Holmes, but he sure had been a good student of Fatty's.

Preeti stood up and waved to Meera. Instinctively, Meera got up too.

'You're also getting off here?' asked Preeti, stuffing her phone into her pocket as she turned to the door.

'Uh...yes,' Meera mumbled, eyeing the large mall outside. 'Meeting friends...'

Malhar inched towards the door behind his sister.

'By the way,' Preeti turned around as the bus come to a halt. 'If you uh...happen to know my aunt and uncle,' she said, scrunching her eyes pleadingly, 'please don't tell them you saw me here.'

24

Love Is in the Air

'Why do you think she said that?' Malhar whispered into Meera's ear, as Preeti threw her bag over her shoulder and strode off towards the sprawling mall.

'Her behaviour is suspicious.' Meera bit her nails.

'Obviously, she wants to hide something!' Malhar's voice was laced with excitement. 'I think Ghosh aunty was right.'

Meera nodded. 'Let's follow her and see what she's here for.'

'See how your cover got blown!' remarked Malhar, as they snaked their way past people waiting at the bus stop and pedestrians on the footpath, tailing Preeti from a safe distance. 'I told you to get a better disguise.'

'Never mind that and focus on her,' Meera stood on tip-toes to track the girl with the green bag, as she merged into a group of people heading into the mall. Running ahead, Meera turned into a large gate that led to a massive compound, then followed Preeti into a corridor lined with potted plants.

'Oye!' Malhar felt a heavy hand pulling him back by his shoulder. 'Kidhar jata hai?'

Wobbling a step or two before finding his balance, Malhar looked up to find a moustached man in a grey uniform holding him back. He pointed to the mall up ahead.

'This is no place for cockroaches like you,' said the security guard, roughing him up by his shoulders.

'I...I my...my didi...' stammered an alarmed Malhar, pointing to a group of people entering the mall. It took him a few seconds to understand why the guard had pulled him up.

'Chal chal,' the guard pushed him towards the footpath. 'Don't show your ugly face here again.'

Malhar felt a wave of anger rising within. Never had he been run roughshod like this before. 'My father is the SSP of Maulsari,' he said, tears stinging his big eyes.

'Wah re Gangu Teli,' laughed the watchman. 'And my grandfather was Raja Bhoj! Get out now before I call the police!'

Go ahead! Call the police! Malhar felt like shouting back. *Then we'll see who has the last laugh!* But rattled and nervous, he didn't find the voice to argue back. Swallowing hard, he turned back, realizing there was no way to get around this. He cursed under his breath. *Why could he not go in?*

Inside, Meera tailed Preeti diligently, like the lamb behind Mary, oblivious to her brother's plight at the gate. Preeti walked down the corridor and turned right. Meera scampered behind her. Preeti got on an escalator. Waiting for a few moments behind a display case to stay out of sight, Meera hopped on too. She got to the next level. But Preeti was nowhere to be seen!

A janitor was sweeping the floor on her right. A salesgirl was arranging neckties in the shop window on the left. It was early and the stores were only just opening. Up ahead, her eyes fell on another escalator. Had Preeti gone to the next level? She looked back. No sign of Malhar. *Where was her silly brother?*

'Tch!' she cursed under her breath and dashed towards the second escalator.

The floor above was like the one below. Sparkling tiles, shining stores, busy cleaners, a handful of salesmen. Meera walked briskly, looking this way and that. And then, from the corner of her eye, spotted an orange kurti inside a coffee shop on her left.

Stepping closer, Meera peered through the glass. It was Preeti alright. She checked again. Her brother was still nowhere to be seen! Pushing open the door, Meera stepped inside, hit by a blast of cold air, pulsating loud music and the aroma of coffee.

Pretending to be looking for someone, Meera's eyes darted every now and then towards Preeti. The girl was chatting with a young boy in a T-shirt and jeans, roughly the same age as her. They were laughing, gazing into each other's eyes, sipping cold coffee from a common glass.

As she watched them, lip-reading their words attentively, Meera was hit by a wave of fatigue; the adrenaline that had kept her going thus far beginning to drain from her veins. She leaned on a high table, her shoulders slumped. *Had all this been a wild-goose chase?*

25

Do Number

The water tank that was as tall as a five-storey building, and the small expanse of open land below it meant many things to the people of Anand Nagar. To children, it was an arena for cricket and football; to women, a breathing space outside their dingy homes; to cart-pullers and labourers, a cool place to catch an afternoon nap; and to jobless ruffians, an adda, or a hang-out spot to while away their hours.

'Kya re fatichar?' Javed put his arm around Mirchi, as they met below the tank that hot summer afternoon. 'What did you steal?'

'O bhai,' Mirchi shrugged off Javed's arm, his eyes on two boys with purple-coloured hair playing carom a few feet away. 'I am not a chor-vor,' he clarified with a wobble of his outstretched fingers. 'I just want to know…'

'What for?' Javed placed a foot on a boulder, then sipped water from his bottle.

'For...uh...increasing knowledge,' Mirchi moved away from the carom players. The last thing he wanted was for word to get around that he was a thief; and word did get around at lightning speed in Anand Nagar.

A fountain of water spurted out of Javed's mouth. 'What, you take me for a fool?' he guffawed.

'Sachi!' Mirchi pressed the skin of his neck. 'God promise!'

'Okay chal.' Javed set the water bottle down and patted the boy, 'What do you want to know?'

'After doing chori, where do chor-log sell the jewellery?'

Javed eyed Mirchi suspiciously. 'You've got the scent?'

Mirchi nodded and tapped his bag.

'Is this also chori-ka-maal?' winked Javed.

'Bola na, I don't do any galat kaam!' Mirchi said emphatically, his eyes darting once again to the carom players.

'Acha chal...so most of the time,' Javed loosened up, 'they sell it to a pawn shop or a jewellery store.'

'So if some aunty's necklace got stolen, she'll find it at the local jewellery shop?'

'Depends,' Javed checked his nails. 'Usually the chor will sell it close to the area where he stole it...but it is unlikely she will find it.'

'Why?'

'Because soon after the maal gets to the pawn shop, the jewellery is broken and taken apart.'

'Matlab?' squinted Mirchi.

'They melt the gold and make something different from...' Javed's words trailed off as his eyes fell upon the large billboard before him. A film star was urging the men of Anand Nagar to abandon fairness creams meant for women and switch to his chosen brand instead, so they could be *real men* like him. Javed tapped on the front-camera of his phone, and grimaced as he examined both sides of his sunburnt face, displeased with what he saw.

'Aage bolega?' Mirchi tugged his arm.

'Abbe ruk,' Javed paused his lesson, then quickly googled to check the price of the star's recommended brand of cream. With a click of his tongue, he slipped the phone back into his pocket. 'Even if that stolen necklace is right before your eyes, you won't recognize it!'

Mirchi pursed his lips. 'Then how do the police find it?'

'They don't!' chuckled Javed.

'Meaning?'

'Tu soch,' Javed said, rolling up the sleeve of his shirt. 'Terrorist attack se mafia don, murder case se festival bandobast—what all will the police do? You think they have time to look for chains and earrings in pawn shops? That too, as soon as the complaint is filed?' he shook his head. 'No chance! Isliye we petty thieves get away. I was never caught!' he boasted, with a tug on his collar. 'In most cases, stolen jewellery is never found. And even if the police find the mudda mal, they gobble it up.'

'Mudda mal?'

'Case property re,' explained Javed. 'Stolen property.'

His eyes fixed on bits of trash paper swirling about in a sudden breeze, Mirchi thought about the burdens on the police force for a moment, but felt little empathy for the khaki-clad men who roughed up good people like Murugan Anna. 'Okay,' he said thoughtfully, as a train clanked past on the tracks behind them. 'Which pawn shops in Maulsari buy stolen jewellery?'

'Look, as you know, I have left this do-number ka kaam,' Javed explained sorrowfully. 'I have promised Rasheeda I won't get back to all this. But I can set you up with my friend Sachin Hathoda. Bhai was into chain-snatching like me, but now he's moved on to big-ticket stuff like construction, extortion,' he said with a tinge of envy in his voice. 'Purana samaan, sikka, painting... kya bolte usko...' he snapped his fingers trying to recall the right word, 'haan, antique! Big money! Hathoda is the only dealer for antiques in all of Maulsari. Maala-mal he's become!'

Mirchi was about to repeat that he doesn't do galat kaam, but stopped short. 'So purana murti-voorti is not melted?'

Fawda shook his head. 'It's value is lost if it's melted.'

'Javed bhai, you are right,' Mirchi grinned sheepishly. 'Actually my friend found some purana maal and wants to find a buyer. Will your Sachin Hathoda help me?'

'Ek scent bottle ke liye itnaich help milega,' Javed slapped Mirchi's back, demanding that he hand over the prize. 'Hathoda bhai ke saath meeting karna hai,' he took a deep breath to inhale the perfume, 'get me some more stuff like this. Then I'll see.'

As Javed slipped the bottle into his pocket, Mirchi smiled, pleased to have Javed in his!

26

Professor in the Picture

Stomach full after a hearty lunch of aamras and puri, Meera flopped on her chair in front of the desktop, pencil hovering over the list of suspects.

'How do *you* know he was her boyfriend?' tittered Malhar, falling flat on the bed behind her. 'As if *you* have a boyfriend!'

Meera turned on the computer. 'Look, I just know more stuff than you, okay? I'm telling you, she lied to her aunt because she was bunking college to go out with her boyfriend. That's why she didn't want me to tell on her. That's all there is to it,' she said, as she opened Google on her computer browser.

'Abhay MITRA'.

More than a million results.

She added two words.

'Abhay MITRA ART HISTORIAN'.

Three hundred thousand results.

'Abhay MITRA ART HISTORIAN MAULSARI'.

Twenty thousand.

'Okay so maybe he is her boyfriend,' Malhar turned to his side and propped himself on his arm. 'What if they planned the robbery together? Remember she kept talking about money on the phone?'

Meera pressed her eyes shut. 'That boy she met wants to get married to her. She wants him to get a job first. That's what it was. I heard them at the coffee-shop! Will you just let it go now?' she said, index finger on mouse, eyes on screen, as she scrolled through the search results. Articles. Pictures. Newspaper links. Interviews. 'This Abhay Mitra is some famous professor,' she mumbled, running over the many titles on art, heritage, and history penned by him.

Malhar exhaled hard and turned away, his eyes drifting from the posters of superheroes and cricketers on the wall to a framed picture from his childhood. He looked at his nine-month-old self, seated on Ma's lap, Baba beaming with a three-year-old Meera on the left, Aaji smiling coyly on the right. It was the day of his home-coming, the day his life had taken a new direction. Thoughts from earlier that morning at the mall returned—being roughed up, shouted at, thrown out. But as the hours had passed, irritation had made way for introspection. *Would life have been like that if Ma and Baba hadn't chosen him to be their son? Was this how people treated Mirchi?* Something stirred inside him.

Behind him, Meera was consumed by her mission, scrutinizing Abhay Mitra's picture closely. Studious round face, wavy, shoulder-length salt-and-pepper hair, rimless glasses, short stubble, light brown eyes... She stopped at the eyes. There was something eccentric, almost sinister, about them. 'This guy looks like Mad-Eye Moody without the eye-patch!' she remarked, reminded of the character in *Harry Potter*. She went back to the search results and scrolled some again.

More articles and interviews. She read the headings of the articles, murmuring softly.

'18 stone idols stolen from ancient temple.'

'Majestic bronze Shiva missing from 500-year-old temple.'

'Customs Officials seize consignment of smuggled idols.'

The news articles seemed puzzling. *People were stealing idols from temples? Why?* With narrowed eyes, she scrolled on, stumbling upon dozens and dozens of new articles either about Mitra or written by him, until a combination of words in one news piece made her miss a breath.

'Oh my god! Oh my god!' she covered her mouth with her hands, as her eyes caught sight of two words beside his name.

'ARRESTED and POLICE'

She clicked open the link, then began reading it aloud.

'Reputed art historian Professor Abhay Mitra was called in for questioning by the police in connection with a missing bronze idol of Goddess Lakshmi from the Royal Heritage Museum. The art conversationist was later taken into police custody. The missing idol is estimated to be worth approximately US $5,50,000 in the art market.'

She snapped her fingers to get Malhar's attention. Turning around on his belly, Malhar looked at his sister, the same thoughts playing in a loop inside his head. *Didi would still have been right here where she is, but where would I have been?*

'Can you see this?' Meera beckoned him closer, her voice charged with anticipation. 'This Mitra person, he has a police case against him for stealing an idol!'

'What?' Malhar broke out of his thoughts and crawled to the foot of the bed.

The siblings exchanged excited glances. After a string of wild-goose chases, perhaps their trail was getting hot after all! Finally, it seemed like their journey had a clear destination. What remained now, was to find the right bus to get there.

27

Back to the Classroom

'I am unable to explain their sudden interest in law,' said Madhavi Pradhan, cracking her knuckles before the principal of Maulsari Law College. 'And this is far easier than answering a hundred and twenty questions every day.'

'As they say,' the principal smiled from behind her desk, 'the apple doesn't fall too far from the tree.'

Thanking the principal, Mrs Pradhan pushed open the door. 'Now remember,' she said to Meera and Malhar seated on a wooden bench outside, as a bell hollered. 'I've got special permission for you to sit in my class. So be quiet and don't disturb the others.'

Walking down a corridor, the siblings followed their mother into a large amphitheatre-like classroom, filled with students.

'Good morning, ma'am,' they rose in unison as Mrs Pradhan greeted them back and walked to a desk in the front.

'So...all ready for the exams next week?' she asked, placing her bag on the table as she signalled for Meera and Malhar to find a place at the back.

Making their way up the wooden steps, Meera observed the students. Some were responding eagerly to their mother's query. Others barely looked up from their phones. Some backbenchers even had their head resting on their desks and were snoring away. *So this is what a college class looks like!*

'Alright,' Mrs Pradhan tucked in the pallu of her saree, then wiped the blackboard. 'This is going to be a revision class. I'll take up your doubts one at a time.'

The room filled with the sound of rustling pages and soft murmurs. Some hands went up.

'Ma'am,' a girl in the front stood up. 'Can you please explain the law related to custody? And,' she added, 'I don't understand the difference between police custody and judicial custody.'

'Custody, as you all know,' began Madhavi Pradhan, gesturing for the girl to be seated, 'is when a person is under another person's control or protection. As you must have studied in your lectures in Constitutional Law, every citizen has a fundamental right to life and liberty. So, nobody can be deprived of those rights, except in a manner provided by the law.'

Some students scribbled into their notebooks. Others listened.

'During the investigation of a case, if the police want to detain a person for questioning or for any other reason, they can keep such a person in their custody, but not for more than twenty-four hours.'

Meera leaned forward, latching on to every word.

'If the police wish to detain a person for more than twenty-four hours,' continued Mrs Pradhan, 'they have to take permission from a magistrate's court. If the magistrate finds good reason, they may permit the police to keep the accused in the police lock-up for upto fifteen days. That is called police custody.'

Pulling out her diary, Meera began taking notes.

'If, however, the investigation is going to take longer or if the police require custody for more than fifteen days, the magistrate may issue an order to keep the accused in jail. This is called judicial custody. Either ways—police custody or judicial custody—if the police detain a person for beyond twenty-four hours, they need a court order. Else it will be regarded as unlawful arrest.'

'But it's been more than twenty-four hours since Velu was arrested,' Malhar nudged Meera. 'You think Inspector Shevre has got this what is it called...order from the magistrate thingy?'

Meera responded with a shrug of her shoulders.

'You think we can ask Baba?' Malhar whispered again, eliciting a stony glare from their mother.

'He will tell us to mind our own business and go pick mangoes.' Meera rolled her eyes, turning her attention to a boy in front who was asking about the various types of offences.

Madhavi Pradhan turned to the blackboard and picked up a white chalk.

'Cognizable,' she wrote on side, and 'Non- cognizable,' she wrote on the other and drew a line between them. 'Cognizable offences are serious like theft, dacoity, murder and so on. In these cases, the police must register an FIR or a First Information Report as soon as they receive a complaint,' she wrote out the points in the first column, 'and can arrest the accused without a warrant from a magistrate. But in the case of non-cognizable offences, the police cannot make an arrest without a warrant.'

Meera copied down the columns verbatim, as did several others.

'So what happened in Mrs Shenoy's house is a cognizable offence,' whispered Malhar, taking his time to put two and two together.

Meera nodded. Next, someone asked about searches.

'If the police suspect a person is hiding stolen property in a certain place, they can conduct a search there after obtaining a search warrant from a magistrate,' explained Mrs Pradhan. 'Two locals, known as panchas, must be called to witness the search, and sign the search-report made up by the police after the search. This report is called a Panchnama.'

Meera remembered Mirchi telling her about the police search at Murugan Plumbing. *Did Shevre have a search warrant? Or had he just landed up there and thrown his weight around?*

'The law further states,' Mrs Pradhan read from a book in her hand, 'that if the police do not have a search warrant, you can refuse them entry into your premises.'

Meera clicked her tongue, wondering how reality could be at such variance with the law. If only Murugan and Velu had known the law, she thought, would they have become sitting ducks before men like Shevre?

Her thoughts were interrupted by the bell. Madhavi Pradhan wished her students well for the exams, before being surrounded by some who had more questions. As the class began emptying out, Meera's eyes caught sight of the college emblem above the board, with a motto inscribed over it in both Sanskrit and English. She'd seen those words on the exam papers her mother brought home to correct, but had never given them a second thought before. But today, they made her sit back and chew on her pencil, as she reflected for the first time, on the import of those lofty words.

Sa Vidya Ya Vimuktaye

Knowledge Liberates

28

With the Blessings of Byomkesh Babu

Right hand on hip, left hand on doorframe, Paromita Ghosh's eyes ran down from Mirchi's dirt-smeared face to his scar-infested feet, then back up to his face. 'E ebar ke?'

'He's Mirchi, the partner we told you about,' Meera introduced the boy. 'You may have seen him taking bhangaar from the building. Mirchi, this is our art teacher.'

Mirchi returned the stare. Bright yellow saree, big red bindi, loopy earrings, glass bangles...*Is she an actress I've seen on TV?* he wondered.

'Ei?' Mrs Ghosh smiled. 'This fellow?'

'Aunty, he's very good in figuring out clues and getting information,' the words poured spontaneously out of Malhar's mouth, eliciting a look of surprise from Meera.

Nodding slightly, Ms Ghosh ushered them in, unable to wrap her head around this strange partnership.

Mirchi stepped in gingerly, gawking at the cane chairs and couches, the bookshelves and paintings. Sauntering in, Malhar deposited himself on a rocking chair, while Meera sat on a sofa, pulling a colourful cushion onto her lap. As Mrs Ghosh switched on lights, Mirchi stared at the crystal lampshades in the tastefully decorated room. Except on one occasion when an elderly woman had called him into her house to collect a heavy pile of newspapers she couldn't carry to the door, Mirchi had never stepped into a home like this.

'Sit,' said Meera.

Mirchi dropped down cross-legged on the mosaic-tiled floor.

'Orree baba,' Mrs Ghosh plonked herself on a sofa. 'Ekhane bosho,' she patted the empty space by her side.

Mirchi stood up, then moved awkwardly towards her, still wondering if she was a celebrity of some sort.

Mrs Ghosh repeated the gesture. 'I am not going to eat you up!' she laughed. 'Murthi will be back from office anytime,' she said, checking the wall clock. 'Then we have to go for the building Ram Navami celebrations downstairs. I'm in charge of the stage decorations, make-up and dressing up the kids participating in the play. And Murthi is playing the role of Narada Muni.'

'I thought it was a children's play,' smiled Meera.

'It is. Children play all the main characters of course. But some of us help. I am the narrator. Harsh, Murthi and some others are doing small roles. Are you all coming?'

Meera nodded. 'They've asked Baba to do some tree-planting or something.'

'Oh yes! Chalo then,' Mrs Ghosh rubbed here palms, 'tell me all that you found out today. I've been waiting! And let's reserve this seat for Byomkesh babu,' she placed a cushion on the cane chair beside her.

The children stared at her in puzzlement.

'You know, they say whenever you narrate stories from the Mahabharata, you must keep a seat for Ashwathama, because he slips in to listen and ensure you're telling the story right. The Chettiers of the south, when they draw up their accounts, they keep a seat for Lord Murugan so he can overview their work. Just like that,' she smiled, 'we shall keep this seat for our Byomkesh babu so his presence can guide us!'

Mirchi stared uncomfortably at the empty chair, half puzzled, half afraid. Malhar beamed; *here was a mystery nut crazier than him!* Meera chuckled, then began recounting the day's events.

As the children took turns to narrate their various exploits, Ms Ghosh's eyes went from curiosity to wonder, and wonder to awe. 'Children, Byomkesh Bakshi is terribly proud of you all.' Then she stood up, walked to the kitchen and brought out a tray of goodies.

'Let's eat.' She set down the tray on a low table and sat down. 'So tell me, how are we to recover the jewels if it's all been melted?'

'Not all,' Mirchi eyed the sweets and snacks. 'They don't melt aunty.'

'Aunty?' the others asked in unison.

'Purana maal,' explained Mirchi. 'Murti, statue, old coin.'

'You mean ANTIQUE?' giggled Meera.

'Haan...wahich!'

'Ei!' Paromita Ghosh held a plate before Mirchi with one hand. 'Ki mishti chhele!' She pinched his cheek with the other. 'You are a sweet fellow.'

Mirchi blushed. He reached out for a samosa, then looked at the cane chair. 'So,' he began with a surge in his confidence, 'tomorrow I giving Fawda this lipstick box Meera giving me,' he patted his bag. 'Then he taking me to Sachin Hathoda who does chori of this purana anti...anti...'

'Ant-eeek,' said Meera slowly.

'Fawda bola, Hathoda bhai only dealer in Maulsari for this anteek-shanteek. So I thinking...if Hathoda bhai only ANT-eek dealer in Maulsari, then Shenoy madam's murti also going...'

'Brilliant!' Mrs Ghosh clapped. 'Mirchi, you are speaking like James Bond! Pakka detective!' she patted him. 'And such a brave boy.' This time she pinched both his cheeks.

Mirchi sat up with straight shoulders, unable to hide the delight on his face. All his life, he'd been told what a duffer he was—a kachrawala, a bhangi, a dirty tramp. To have a pretty memsahib shower him with such unbridled praise made his head spin.

'Who knows?' Mrs Ghosh bit into a kachori. 'This Hathdoda fellow himself may have Shenoy's murti. If not the jewels, at least we can track down the idol that is so precious to her.'

'Exactly,' Meera snapped her fingers. 'That's what we were thinking too. But before Mirchi can meet Hathoda,' she said, 'we need your help.'

29

An Artful Operation

Seated in a sea of photo albums in the living room, Mrs Ghosh adjusted her glasses. 'This was twelve years ago. Our vacation in Ooty and Coimbatore.' She tapped a picture.

'You look so young in these photos!' squealed Meera, tucking her feet under her.

'These are you children?' asked Malhar, pointing to a young girl smiling coyly behind a rose bush and a taller boy by her side.

'Aparajita and Ajoy,' nodded Mrs Ghosh, kissing the picture. 'Apu left for college last year, but she'll be coming for the summer holidays next month. And Ajoy is studying abroad. Okay, so let's see what we have here,' she sighed and turned a page. 'Look at this murti of Hanuman.'

'But it's partly covered by your daughter's hand,' said Meera, her head at a tilt.

'Oh this one!' Malhar pointed to a statue of Shiva and Parvati.

'It's a bit hazy,' Mrs Ghosh shook her head.

Mirchi gazed at the pictures from the Ajanta and Ellora caves to the majestic Brihadeshwara temple, the stunning Sun temple in Konarak and of the world-famous Taj Mahal. He'd only ever seen these on TV.

'Got it!' Mrs Ghosh extracted a photo from underneath the plastic cover. 'This Ganesha will be perfect,' she said. 'See usually, Ganpathi's trunk is on his left but in this one, it is to the right. So this will make it look like you've laid your hands on a very rare murti. It will get Hathoda to talk.'

The children peered at the statue in the picture; it appeared to be on the outer wall of a temple. Mrs Ghosh reached out for her mobile phone and clicked a picture of the picture. Then she got up, walked over to her laptop on a side-table, with the children tagging along behind her. 'Now,' she said, opening up the picture in an application, 'let's remove the background.' She hummed a tune as she tapped some buttons on her screen. Suddenly the original background was gone, and replaced with something else.

'Wow!' Meera exclaimed, as she watched the picture take on a new avatar.

'No, not this one. It looks a bit strange, nai? Let's try this.' Mrs Ghosh tapped on some other icons.

'This is so cool!' Malhar's eyes grew large as he watched his art teacher tinker with colour, tone, brightness and a bunch of other things. 'When I grow up, I'm going to have my own detective business,' he set off on his usual refrain, 'and get this software!'

'Eh...I use this for my design projects,' winked Mrs Ghosh. 'But yes, it doesn't hurt to find a new use for it.'

Gawking unblinkingly at the screen, Mirchi jumped in alarm as the printer by his knee spluttered on.

'There you are,' Mrs Ghosh handed the printout to Mirchi. 'Now you tell this Hathoda fellow that your friend has this murti and that he stole it from a temple and wants to sell it. It will help you befriend him. Maybe he will then give you some information which might help us.'

Mirchi nodded, overwhelmed by the electric speed at which this operation had been put together.

'But be careful. These smugglers can be dangerous and—'

The door burst open and a man entered with jingling keys.

'Hello Murthi uncle,' Meera and Malhar greeted the man. 'That's Ghosh aunty's husband.' Malhar whispered to Mirchi.

'Idhar bhi murti, udhar bhi Murthi!' snickered Mirchi, looking up from the printout.

'Why so late?' Mrs Ghosh asked her husband.

'Don't ask,' Mr Murthi sighed, waving to the children, then flopping on a stool. 'A big scam has broken out at the bank. We're all having to do extra time to piece the whole paper trail together.'

'Scam?' asked Malhar excitedly. 'So have you found the thief?'

'Oh we have some suspects but it's a long process. First one must find out the facts, only then can one arrive at some conclusion. In a proper investigation, one's theories must be based on facts,' he smiled. 'Not facts on theories!'

Meera played out the words in her head, then shrugged, unsure what they really meant.

'So...art class over?' asked Mr Murthi, untying his shoelaces.

'Eh...no art class today.' Mrs Ghosh got up from her seat. 'We are also trying to solve a scam,' she winked, returning to the kitchen. 'Today, the kids have only been talking and talking...about the theft in our building.'

'Ah, what's happening in that case?' Mr Murthi stuffed his socks into his shoes, then stretched out his toes. 'Have the police found the thief?'

'Not yet,' replied Meera.

'Poor chap that Harsh Shenoy.' Mr Murthi placed his shoes on the rack and sank into a sofa, as Mrs Ghosh brought him a steaming cup of tea, then disappeared again into another room. 'First his business took a big hit during COVID. And now this! He came to meet me at the bank last month to know how to adjust his home loan as he's having trouble repaying it. Poor man! It's really unfortunate how trouble begets more trouble. You know in Tamil we have a saying: a broken house will keep breaking, an injured hand will keep getting hurt.'

'Uncle,' said Meera. 'You know Tamil?'

'Naturally,' Mr Murthi slurped his tea, 'it's my mother tongue.'

'So...' she pulled out her diary. 'What is the meaning of...this word—kaapa?

'Kaapa?'

'Yeah, it sounds something like car park,' said Meera. 'I heard someone in trouble shouting to his uncle "Mama Car Park" or something like that.'

'Oh you mean kaapaathu?' laughed Murthi, setting down his cup.

'Yes,' Meera nodded. 'Exactly!'

'Car park!' chuckled Mrs Ghosh, emerging from the bedroom. 'This is just like your aunty for antique.' She nudged Mirchi fondly.

Meera grimaced. 'I didn't mean to be mean,' she said to Mirchi, 'by laughing at you earlier.'

Basking in all the attention and affection he was getting from Mrs Ghosh, Mirchi brushed it away. Hardened by caste slurs and accustomed to expletives, Meera's laughter had caused him no offence at all; in fact he'd barely registered it.

'Kaapathu means bachao,' replied Mr Murthi. 'The fellow you heard was asking for help. Help me, help me! By the way, who is this boy?' he suddenly noticed Mirchi. 'New student?'

'Oh long story.' Mrs Ghosh rounded up the children and herded them to the door. 'Now we have to get going for the function. I'll tell you later. And Mirchi,' she handed the boy a bag, 'there's some soap, shampoo and two of Ajoy's outgrown shirts and jeans in here. Go well-dressed for your meeting tomorrow.' She held up two thumbs. 'Work your magic on Hathoda!'

30

A Theatrical Exposé

'Alright sir, you may begin,' Arun Shekhar, the balding secretary of Customs Colony came hurrying up with a cameraman. 'Rahu-kala is over. Now it is an auspicious time to do the planting.'

Overlooking the large group of residents gathered around him at the back of the colony, the SSP nodded, then reached out for the mahua sapling and carefully placed it inside a pit in the ground. Patting it firmly into place, he took a small spade and covered up its roots with mud.

Onlookers clapped, some took pictures. Others chanted Jai Shri Ram as the sound of dhol rented the air.

'This tree above us,' smiled the secretary, pointing to the fragrant maulsari above them, 'was planted by my grandfather on the occasion of Ram Navami fifty years ago. It is a practice we have been following for years, and it is an honour for us all to have our SSP join us in this noble endeavour today.'

'This is such a wonderful tradition you follow here,' smiled Madhavi Pradhan, looking around the thicket.

The secretary ushered them towards a large pandal at the centre. 'Please join us for the play our colony children have prepared specially for this day. Every year they work very hard to put this up. Then we have a puja, followed by dinner. I hope you have time to stay till the end.'

'Most certainly,' nodded the SSP as Aaji and Mrs Pradhan headed off to speak to some others and Malhar sneaked off to sniff out the snacks.

As Meera walked with her dad towards the pandal slowly, she decided to let out the question that had been troubling her. 'Baba, why do the police beat up suspects after arresting them?'

Taken aback, SSP Pradhan turned his alarmed eyes to Meera.

'It's nothing actually,' Meera explained. 'I saw something in a movie.'

'Hmmm... Yes, it is true that on some occasions the police go beyond the measures they are permitted to take while conducting an investigation. But keep in mind, that they are doing a very tough job. Often, policemen work under extremely trying and stressful conditions that too, with limited resources. They are responsible to maintain law and order...there are all kinds of pressures. So yes, perhaps there are a few occasions when the police go overboard. But I would like to think they are an exception rather than the norm.'

'But,' Meera interjected, itching to tell her father what she'd seen and heard at the chowki, but was nudged out by Mr Shekhar and a host of other residents, eager to meet her father.

'This is Mr Bharat Iyer from B-12,' Mr Shekhar introduced a middle-aged man. 'He is with the Income Tax Department.'

'Hello, sir. Glad to meet you. I am Kavita Balakrishna from A-2 building, General Manager, Co-operative Bank of Maulsari.' A lady hustled forward.

'Hello, sir...hello, sir...hello, sir...' grunted Meera, dropping down on a plastic chair and crossing her hands before her, tired of all the people eager to meet and greet her father. 'We hardly get any time with Baba and the one day that he comes early he has to meet some forty thousand people!'

'And this is Harsh Shenoy from A-3, the chief anchor of our society.'

Meera spun around, got up and stood beside her father as Malhar dawdled towards them with a bowl of snacks.

Stopping before the SSP, Harsh nodded, his hands occupied with a basket filled with all sorts of props from maces to crowns and turbans to wigs.

'The Shenoys are always at the heart of every colony event,' Mr Shekhar continued. 'Even now, despite all the tension in their house, Mrs Shenoy is leading the bhajan-singing.' He pointed to the stage decked with diyas and flowers. 'And Harsh is helping with the play.'

'Hello, sir,' Harsh Shenoy, dressed in a saffron silk kurta and yellow stole, smiled slightly, the dark circles under his eyes even more prominent now than when Meera had met him at the temple.

'I agree with Shekhar,' cut in Mrs Balakrishna. 'No society event is complete without them. Ganpathi, Diwali, Dussehra—their family is always there in full cheer. Such good souls I tell you. So respectful and dignified despite all their troubles.'

'Hello, Harsh,' SSP Pradhan smiled. 'Your father met me last week as I was on my way to office. It's good to meet you. Please let your father know that after we spoke, I had a word with the SHO of the local police station who's in charge of this investigation. He's assured me he is doing everything he can to get to the bottom of this theft.'

'It's all destiny!' Harsh looked skyward, taking the same lofty view of things as his mother. 'I'd told my mother to put the jewels in the bank locker,' he said with a regretful shake of his head. 'But she said she'd put them away after a function the following week,' he sighed. 'All a play of destiny!'

Meera scowled. *Wait! That's not what his mother had said!* She looked at Malhar, but the boy was busy ogling at Harsh's Rolex, spinning about to admire it from all angles, even as he stuffed his face with halwa. *And wait!* She turned to her Baba. Was the *word* from her dad, the *pressure* on Inspector Shevre to beat up Velu? Was the poor plumber getting socked in the lock-up because of a casual phone call from Baba? She swallowed hard. Even the thought seemed unsettling.

'Harsh uncle.' A boy dressed like Hanuman came hurrying along. 'We need the props backstage. The play is about to start.'

'I need to get going,' said Harsh, holding up the basket in his hand as an explanation. 'Please excuse me.' He walked off towards the stage.

Arun Shekhar led SSP Pradhan to a row of chairs in front, as Mrs Shenoy's bhajan group exited the stage and children dressed as Rama, Sita, Hanuman and an array of characters from the Ramayana strode on. The lights became dim as Meera and Malhar settled down beside their father and a single beam of light shone upon a rishi on the front of the stage, in a flowing white beard and long white hair.

'That's Harsh uncle, isn't it?' said Malhar, noticing his saffron kurta. 'He's Rishi Valmiki I guess.'

'Shenoy aunty's make-up skills are excellent,' smiled Meera.

'And that...that Narada Muni is Murthi uncle,' chuckled Malhar, as their art teacher's husband appeared with a top-knot over his head, and veena in his hand.

'He looks cute,' Meera smiled, as for the next few hours their mystery lay forgotten at the altar of an evergreen epic.

31

The Hammer

Born the day Sachin Tendulkar had hit a smashing century in a one-day match, his parents had had no difficulty in finding their son a suitable name. But trading bat for hammer, the burly giant of a man towering before Mirchi, had acquired for himself a second name that paid obeisance to his prowess with the tool of his choice—Hathoda.

'Salaam bhai,' Javed raised his hand respectfully before his former colleague who had now risen to greater heights. 'As I told you on the phone, this chirkut has some work for you,' he nudged Mirchi forward before the plastic desk under a makeshift shelter, in the centre of the construction site. To his left was a mountain of cement, on his left a pile of bricks. A concrete mixer tumbled at the back while over a dozen under-nourished women milled about carrying materials on their head.

Face glowing, hair shining, dressed smartly in a light blue shirt and jeans, Mirchi noticed Hathoda's beefy arm, the thick gold chain on his neck, the fancy sunglasses on his head.

'Jaldi bol,' said the giant-man, licking his finger as he counted a wad of notes.

'I...uh..have...uh,' Mirchi stuttered.

'Bol,' said Hathoda impatiently. 'Kya item hai?'

'Bhagwan ki murti,' replied Mirchi.

'Metal? Stone?'

'Uh...stone...'

'Size?'

Mirchi displayed the face of his palm.

'How old?'

Mirchi shrugged. Clearly this Hathoda fellow didn't waste his time on idle talk. Chances of befriending him and extracting information from him, like he had done with Fawda, seemed bleak.

'Hundred? Two hundred? Five hundred years?'

Mirchi shrugged again.

'Kidhar mila?'

'Uh...mandir...on hill...inside forest...near my gaon.'

For the first time since he'd arrived, Hathoda looked up from the notes, at Mirchi's face, then eyed the boy's stick-like arms, then his scrawny legs.

'My cousin,' said Mirchi quickly, getting the drift of Hathoda's puzzled gaze. 'He broke it from temple. I was just helping.'

Hathoda nodded knowingly. The Indian countryside was dotted with ancient temples and abandoned ruins. It sounded like a plausible explanation.

'Photo hai?' Hathoda tied the notes into a rubber band and slipped them into a metal box on the desk.

Mirchi extracted the printout from his pocket, unfolded it and placed it on the white table.

Hathoda picked it up and took a quick look. Then he placed it back down, picked up his phone, asked Fawda to step aside to allow the light through, and clicked a picture. Then he began tapping something on his phone.

'You sending photo to your boss?' Mirchi tried to peek into the device, eager to know the ultimate source of this business. He felt a sharp pinch on his shoulder; a signal from Fawda to stay quiet, and speak only when spoken to.

Hathoda said nothing, turning his eyes to the workers and barking instructions to someone at the back. In less than a minute, his phone pinged. He looked at it, then turned to Michi. 'Where is the murti now?'

'I can't tell you,' said Mirchi, mustering up all the courage at his disposal. 'I only tell the dealer.'

'Abbe gadhe!' Hathoda reached across the desk and caught hold of Mirchi by the scruff of his neck. 'I am the dealer!'

Mirchi could hear his heart pounding; but he held tight to his cloak of calmness. 'No. I mean the bada sahab, whoever is going to pay. Who you message...' he said, trying to appear unflustered. Having grown up the way he had, Mirchi had enough of a street sense to know that Hathoda's interest in him was only until he'd laid his hands on the idol. After that, this giant-man would have little use for him. He was also astute enough to understand that Hathoda had sent the picture to someone higher up, and that person had replied conveying an interest in the murti.

Hathoda let go of Mirchi, then fixed both him and Fawda with an intimidating stare. His phone began ringing. He answered it, speaking first in monosyllables then in short sentences. Mirchi could not understand because it was in a language he could not follow. But even though the words were incomprehensible, he could tell from the tone of his voice and Hathoda's roving eyes on him, that the person on the other end, whoever it was, was not just interested—he was very interested! Mrs Ghosh had selected well.

'Look, if you don't want it, I'll go ask someone else,' said Mirchi with a mask of confidence. He took back his picture and put it into his pocket once Hathoda hung up his call.

Fawda stared after him, partly in awe, partly in dread.

'Oye Dhapu!' Hathoda called out. 'Chal, I take you to dealer. But seventy per cent mera.'

'Seventy?' Mirchi made big eyes. 'Tch' he clicked his tongue and turned to leave, to give his act an air of authenticity. The giant-man was in, the ball was now in his court.

'Okay chal, tu Fawda ka dost hai. For you I'll do for fifty per cent.'

Fawda stared at Mirchi with new-found respect. The boy had the guts to haggle with Hathoda? And was pulling it off?

Mirchi didn't turn back, only held up two fingers to signify the commission he was willing to part with. He knew the ways of the world, and rarely if ever, did blokes like him have an upper hand in anything. He savoured the moment.

'Okay, thirty...last...' Hathoda stood up. 'I won't do it for less! Nobody will.'

Mirchi turned around, walked back to the table and slapped Hathoda's hand. 'Deal!'

•

32

Dugout Discussions

'Arre how I supposed to know? I only wanting to make friendship with him,' said Mirchi, as he carted out yet another rusted cycle from Meera and Malhar's school's cluttered backyard. 'But he sending picture to his boss and his boss very interested in murti. He wanting to see. And Hathoda taking me to meet boss in afternoon! What I do now?'

'This is fantastic!' Malhar's eyes sparkled with envy. How he wished he, too, could go into a smuggler's den.

'Not fantastic,' Meera coughed, as she brought out a cardboard box filled with broken lamps. 'What will he show him? The same photo again?'

'Ghanta!' Mirchi put the cycle on its stand under a tree, threw down his bag and plonked himself beside Munna. 'Now he going to find out that I'm feku-singh, and making kheema out of me.' He pretended to chop, holding one palm at right angles over the other. 'You should have seen his arms! Each dus kilo ka—like tree-trunks!'

'Wait,' Meera waved to the school-watchman who had grown mighty pleased with their sincere efforts in clearing up the junk at the back of the school, then placed the box on the back of the cycle, as Munna trudged along. 'There must be some way around this.'

'Guys, by the way, what about Preeti?' Malhar tied the box to the carrier. 'Are we going to stop checking up on her?'

'Tch,' Mirchi pulled his knees closer and tucked them under his arms. 'Preeti no doing chori.'

'How can you be so sure?' Malhar rested his hand on his hip.

'Dekh,' Mirchi scrunched his eyes against the sun's glare. 'Say it is school-time, but you no going school. You going maidan for cricket-wicket. That time, Ghosh aunty and Murthi uncle seeing you. What you doing?'

'I...uh,' Malhar postulated, 'I'd tell them not to tell Ma and Baba that I had bunked school.'

'Haan!' Mirchi slapped his palm with the back of the other. 'Now if you are chor,' he continued. 'And they finding you in wrong place. You saying hello aunty, hello uncle with big smile? Or you hiding?'

'Hmmm,' nodded Meera knowingly, getting the drift of Mirchi's deduction. 'That's a good point. When she saw me, *she* turned around and said hi first. And she sounded very casual and chilled.'

'My dadi always saying, chor ke daadi mein tinka,' Mirchi persisted. 'Meaning—'

'—Meaning a guilty person cannot hide their guilt. I know, I know,' nodded Malhar. 'And what about Sarla's husband?'

'Arre haan,' Mirchi snapped his fingers. 'You asking me to check about Ali baba so I checking.'

'Ali Baba?'

Mirchi scratched his head. 'Ali. You saying na that day...'

'You mean alibi?'

'Haan! He having some liver-shiver problem. That full day Yeda Raghu in hospital. My cousin, Bheja-Fry, who was in same hospital that day with his dadi, telling me Bewda Raghu, akha din, behosh on bed.' Mirchi stuck out his tongue and spread out his hands and feet, pretending to be comatose.

'Bheja-Fry,' snickered Malhar. 'What a name!' Then his face lit up with an idea. 'Hey! When you go to meet Hathoda, why don't you say the murti is with your cousin in the gaon? That you need more time to bring it here?'

'Good idea,' Meera dusted her palms. 'Tell him you can arrange to get it once you know the price.'

'Haan,' Mirchi patted Malhar. 'Yeh super-duper idea hai.'

'Where do you have to meet Hathoda?' asked Meera.

Mirchi extracted a crumpled piece of paper from his pocket and gave it to her.

‘Savera Industries, Maulsari EPZ,’ she read from it. ‘It seems like the industrial area in the export promotion zone. Do you know that locality? Are you sure it’s safe?’

‘We’ll come with you,’ Malhar jumped in.

‘Arre it’s not a shaadi!’ Mirchi said through crinkled eyes. ‘Hathoda won’t let me in with a baraat na...’

‘We won’t join you, but stay close behind.’ Meera tightened the knots Malhar had tied. ‘Just in case you need help. And you know what? I’ll borrow Aaji’s phone for one afternoon and give it to you, in case of an emergency. I’ll set Ghosh aunty’s number on fast-dial. You call her in case of a problem.’

‘And if you can’t speak,’ said Malhar, excited to put together a contingency plan, ‘just give a missed call. Let the phone ring twice and cut it. That will be signal that you need help. We’ll tell Ghosh aunty about it. When you go in, we will follow you up to a point and wait somewhere close by—Meera, Munna and me, just in case...’

‘Dekh Munna, dadi always right!’ Mirchi mounted the cycle, to take the day’s collection to Aslam Chacha’s kabadi shop as Munna trotted behind him. ‘I becoming bada aadmi already,’ he beamed. ‘I having bodyguard! Ek nahi...two two!’ He winked at his partners, then pedalled away with a whistle and a smile.

33

Marching In

Finding a suitable spot towards one end of the street, Meera signalled to Malhar to get behind the enormous rain tree, Munna staying by her knee. It seemed like a quiet place, in the small lane flanked by high factory walls. From here, they could keep an eye on Mirchi at the other end of the street, and stay reasonably well concealed in the narrow space between the huge brown trunk and drab grey wall. Only a few days ago, their bus had snaked through the industrial part of the city as they'd chased Preeti. Little did they know then that the dockyard area dotted with warehouses and cranes was to become the hub of their mystery.

A van spluttered past them and turned into a compound, beyond which Mirchi was seated on a platform under the shade of a massive peepal tree, staring at the large gate before him with a sign board pinned over its archway.

SAVERA GROUP OF INDUSTRIES

SAVERA MARBLES

SAVERA GAS

SAVERA COSMETICS

'Why has Hathoda called him here?' asked Malhar scanning the names on the signboard at the far end. 'It's a marble factory, and they also make cosmetics. And what is the meaning of gas? As in gas cylinders?'

'No clue,' Meera noted down the names in her diary, then held her camera to her eye and focused on the signboard above the partially open factory gate. CLICK CLICK.

'Oye!' a voice startled them. They turned around to find a paan-chewing watchman speaking to them from a small opening in the wall behind them that they hadn't noticed before. 'Kya hai?'

Malhar swallowed hard, reminded of his bitter experience with the watchman at the mall. Meera took a step forward, prepared to deliver the lines she'd rehearsed for exactly such a situation.

'Baba...office,' she pointed vaguely to a warehouse someplace in the distance, hoping that would be sufficient to turn the man away. 'School vacation...'

Not convinced, he stepped toward them, eying them with suspicion. 'Kaunsa office?' he pulled his belt over his belly.

'Mehta Electricals,' replied Meera confidently, having checked out the names of nearby enterprises on Google Maps.

'Idhar kya kaam hai?'

'Drawing,' Meera tapped her diary, pointed to a magpie robin on the tree above them, then to her camera. 'Pakshi.'

The watchman nodded pensively then turned away.

It was surprising how much they could get away with because they were kids, Meera thought to herself. Surely, children would make for the best spies and detectives! 'We'll have to move to another spot after some time,' she said, 'but without giving Mirchi away,' as the gate to Savera Enterprises opened to let out a tempo loaded with slabs of granite. Mirchi stood up, approached the open gate, then peeped in on tiptoes. A watchman marched towards him, they spoke, he turned back to close the gate, and Mirchi returned to his waiting spot under the peepal.

Scampering on, Meera and Malhar settled by a row of parked trucks ahead, wincing at the stench of urine along the wall. A man was snoring in one truck, but the others seemed empty. Finding a quiet spot, Meera stopped, then peeped out from behind the truck.

A bike roared past them towards the gate of Savera Enterprises. The rider was a beefy man with stylish sunglasses. Raising his arm, Mirchi called out to the rider. Then he ran up to him.

'That must be Sachin Hathoda,' mumbled Malhar, crouching beside Meera.

'Hmmm,' Meera held her breath. CLICK CLICK.

'BHOW BHOW! WOOF WOOF! BHOW BHOW!

A stray that had been sleeping under the shade of the parked trucks began barking.

'Shh...Shhh Shhhh...' Malhar rummaged in his bag for biscuits so he could befriend the dog and buy its silence. But he couldn't find any.

'Grrr...' Munna grunted, barring his teeth. Then he let out a volley of barks. Not to be intimidated by an outsider in it's turf, the other dog responded with aggressive barks. But Munna was having none of it. He stood his ground, and let out a deep growl, securing Meera and Malhar like a shield.

Disturbed by the noise, the sleeping man in the truck, who'd been as still as a log of wood so far, began to stir. The watchman of Savera Enterprises started looking their way, curious about the commotion.

Heart pounding, eyes on Mirchi, Meera's hands trembled as she tried taking another picture from behind the truck. *Would this noise give them away and jeopardize Mirchi?* She noticed Hathoda telling the watchman something, who then waved Mirchi through the gate. She managed another shot as the barking contest began to ebb. The other dog was backing off, giving in to Munna. Much to her relief, the sleeping man turned on his side and was snoring away in seconds. The curious watchman, having let Mirchi through, returned to his kiosk.

'You're the best, Munna,' Malhar rubbed the dog's sides, as they watched the gate close in behind Mirchi. 'Cream biscuits for you tomorrow!'

34

Into the Lion's Lair

Making his way into the metal gate, Mirchi found himself in a large compound. In front of him arose a wide-faced single-storey factory building; to his right was a ground filled with parked two-wheelers and cars, including a posh-looking white car; and to his left, a series of tin sheds extending all the way to the back of the compound, along the side of the building. Workmen and loaders pottered about the premises, but Hathoda was nowhere to be seen.

Taking small steps, Mirchi advanced towards the tin sheds, a tad intimated to enter the imposing factory. He saw slabs of black granite in a parked tempo, another stacked with white marble, a third had rows of gas cylinders. As he walked along, in the passage between the sheds and the building, he noticed a side-door to the factory and was drawn in by a strong scent. Stepping through the little door, he found himself on a metal bridge along the inner wall of the building, overlooking the shop floor of a massive factory. Below him, machines whirred away, cutting, crushing, and compressing. Puffs of steam rose at one end, neat bars of soap emerged smoothly in a line into a conveyor belt at the other. 'Dekh, Munna,' Mirchi mumbled, 'this is soap factory.'

He heard a rush of footsteps behind him, then a heavy hand on his shoulder. 'What are you doing here?' A short fellow with a hideous gash across his left eye, stood over him.

Mirchi stared at the stranger.

'Tu Mirchi hai?'

Mirchi nodded.

'Toh chal!' The man caught hold of him and pulled him out of the door. 'Hathoda bhai is looking for you.'

Mirchi followed the man along the side of the building towards the back, wondering if Hathoda's assistant would be more of a talker than his boss.

'Akku bhai,' a loader placing gas cylinders on a trolley by the side, patted the man. 'Kab aaya sasural se? Bail done?'

Mirchi's escort gave the man a friendly pat, held up his thumb, then walked on.

Mirchi swallowed hard, staring at the trolley. He knew from casual chit-chat with Fawda that criminals referred to jail as their sasural or in-law's home, because they were such regular visitors. So it meant the man walking before him had just come out of jail!

But what startled him even more were the cylinders on the trolley. They were all cut in half! He'd never seen anything like that before.

Rounding the back of the building past sounds of cutting and drilling, Akku bhai lead Mirchi into a smaller building behind the main building, guarded by a beefy watchman standing before a heavy metal gate. Akku gave him a nod, the guard stepped aside and pushed open the door for them. As they stepped in, Mirchi missed a breath. Because the soap factory had transformed into Ali Baba's cave, filled with all kinds of exotic antiquities!

They walked past a large stone Nandi on the floor. Then a statue of Ganesha nearly as tall as him. A murti with a crack on the hand that Mirchi couldn't recognize. He stared at it for a moment; *was it a woman or a man*? He couldn't tell. He walked on with a shrug to spot a glimmering shiv-linga. Then a grey stone elephant. A sitting Buddha. A reclining Vishnu. Temple bells. Amphora jugs. Exquisitely carved stone pillars. Ornamental panels. Mirchi couldn't believe what he was seeing. 'Yeh sab kya hai?' he mumbled.

Akku bhai ambled on without replying.

'Yeh kidhar se aaya?' Mirchi persisted.

'Tu kya socha?' Akku bhai chuckled. 'You're the only one doing this chori?'

Mirchi paused beside a striking statue of Shiva and ran his finger over the stone.

'Aye! No touching,' Akku bhai gave Mirchi a thwack on his back. 'Karodon ka maal hai!'

'Karod?' Mirchi's eyes grew large.

'Ammer log in Amreeca...Swissland...' Akku bhai rubbed his thumb and forefinger together to convey money. 'Keeping statue in house, in showcase, in garden.'

Mirchi scratched his head, wondering what he'd do if ever he were to have crores of rupees. Clearly getting statues like these wouldn't figure in the list. But before he could work out his answer, a wave of dread washed over him. It occurred to him that if this whole business was indeed worth so much, if anyone were to find out his true motive for being here, that would be the end of him.

In an enclosure by the side, his eye spotted smaller sculptures made of wood, bronze and ivory. His heartbeat quickened as his eyes scanned them like a hawk, hoping to spot Mrs Shenoy's murti amongst the lot. He noticed some ganeshas, a few tall lamps, some elephants, a flying Hanuman.

And then it dawned upon him! How stupid of him, to show up here expecting to stumble upon the stolen statue. This was like looking for a needle in a haystack. And to add to his woes, he simply had no idea what kind of needle he was looking for! He cursed himself, as the extent of his foolishness hit him. *What on earth did a Mahalsa Devi murti look like?*

35

A Strange Visitor

'It's getting boring!' sighed Malhar turning back to look at the factory gate for the umpteenth time. It had been over half an hour since Mirchi had gone in. Except an occasional vehicle and some buzzing flies, little moved on the quiet street. 'When is he going to come out?'

Meera had her eyes on a passing car that stopped at the street corner to dump some trash onto a mountain of garbage, before driving off. How odd that people called Mirchi filthy, she thought, when he was the one cleaning the filth and they were the ones creating it!

'You think something may have gone wrong?' Malhar cut into her thoughts, holding out a packet of chewing gum before his sister.

Meera took it, eyeing yet another car that had entered the street. This one was bigger and drove right up to the gate of the Savera Factory and honked twice. The watchman who'd let Mirchi through, came scampering towards the car. The dark glass of the rear window rolled down to reveal the face of a moustached man.

'Haven't we seen him before?' Meera scrunched her eyes.

Malhar unwrapped the gum and peered at the car.

The man took off his sunglasses as he spoke and placed them over his head. The guard saluted and waved him through. Dabbing his forehead thrice with his handkerchief, the man in the car held up his hand, as the watchman threw open the gate.

'Oh my god, oh my god, oh my god! Meera exclaimed, reminded of the gesture, 'That's that's...Baba's friend....

'The Rajnikanth fan,' Malhar caught on. 'Aaji's brinjal face! Uh...something like Samar—Samir! Samir Naik!'

'Yes yes yes! He's some Deputy Commissioner or something!'

'What's he doing here?'

'What if he's here to raid this place? Oh my god, Mirchi is inside!' Meera held her head in her hands.

'But he told Baba that he is on leave,' Malhar reminded his sister. 'How can he be here for a raid? And how can he raid the place alone? Wouldn't he come with a team?' Malhar countered his sister's anxiety with cold reason.

Meera nodded, then shrugged. Too many questions. No clear answers.

CLICK.

CLICK.

She managed two shots of the man before he rolled up his tinted glass and the car sped into the gate.

'This is just so....' Meera held her head, 'bizarre-random!' she sighed, feeling much like a girl named Alice who'd gone down a rabbit hole and exclaimed—curiouser and curiouser!

36
Big Boss

Akku bhai sauntered past another metal door into a walled enclosure, deposited Mirchi beside Hathoda with a grunt, and turned away.

Looking up briefly from his phone, Hathoda pointed Mirchi to a balding man in a brown safari suit. 'Daya sa'ab.'

Mirchi stared at the sahib who was peering through a magnifying lens at coins in a felt-covered tray. Shuffling on his feet, Mirchi thought it curious that he'd imagined the big boss to be a quintessential smuggler from the movies—pockmarked face, thick paan-stained lips, bloodshot eyes, beefy arms, gold watch, thick chain. But the man before him did not fit into that template at all. He seemed like the friendly neighbourhood uncle, the sort who couldn't harm a fly.

His eyes darted towards a white man in a thin cotton shirt and beige shorts, peering into a thick catalogue book at a desk to one side. Was this gora sahab one of the rich people from Amreeca that Akku bhai had just mentioned? The man hadn't noticed Mirchi: he seemed to be in a world of his own.

Looking up from the tray after a few minutes, the sahib turned to Mirchi. 'So...Chotu...' he beckoned the boy toward him. 'You're the fellow with the Ganesha?'

Mirchi nodded, his eyes roving over the coins in the tray. Silver, copper, round, square, some with holes and marks, others with signs and letters. Some had images of warriors, others of gods.

'It's a rare one. Where did you find it?'

'In mandir near my gaon sa'ab,' said Mirchi.

'Kaise toda?' he put aside the tray and wiggled Mirchi's thin arms.

'Uh...crowbar,' Mirchi mumbled. 'My big brother in village...he breaking. I only helping,' he nodded, realizing his wiry frame didn't do much to evince confidence in his stone-breaking abilities. 'He very tagda aadmi, just like Hathoda sa'ab.'

'Hmm...this temple,' the man tapped open the picture on his phone, 'where exactly is it?'

'Jungle mein hai sa'ab,' replied Mirchi, trying to keep things ambiguous, his eyes darting about a glass cabinet with smaller bronze idols. He spotted some goddess-like figures, but just couldn't tell one from the other.

'People still go there to pray?'

'Nahi sa'ab...it is inside ghana jungle.'

The input seemed to please the man. 'How many can you bring?'

Mirchi narrowed his eyes. 'Yeh...ek murti hai,' he extracted the printout from his pocket.

Hathoda tapped Mirchi on the head. 'Sa'ab has seen this. He's asking if you can bring more!'

'Jee, sa'ab,' Mirchi bobbed his head, 'I telling my cousin. He bringing.'

'First, tell your cousin to go there and take some photos,' said the boss-man. 'Have them sent to me.' He gave Hathoda an instructional glare. 'I will tell you which ones you should break.'

'Sa'ab...kitna dega?' Mirchi kept up the pretence, apparent to him now that this was no quick-flash T-20 but a long-hauling Test match. Perhaps if he got another chance to come back here with a clearer idea of what this Mahalsa Devi looked like, he might be able to trace Mrs Shenoy's stolen idol.

'Daya sa'ab,' Akku popped his head in, 'Sir aaya hai.'

The boss-man stood up and patted Mirchi. 'Don't worry about all that. You'll be well compensated. Do as I say first, and get me more photos. Clear hai?'

Mirchi gave a slight nod as a large-framed moustached man sailed into the enclosure. And then he watched in amazement as the boss-man transformed from lion to mouse before the visitor. Suddenly, there was frenzied activity. A boy brought in chairs, someone else carried in a floor-fan, instructions were sent out for tea and snacks for the bada-sahib, people went scurrying about briskly in all directions. Mirchi looked on as Daya sahib shook hands with the big man, and then they hugged.

'Oye!' he felt a heavy hand on his shoulder. 'Fut idhar se!' said Hathoda with a flick of his fingers. 'Get the photos, then come and meet me,' he instructed Mirchi, then told him it was time for him to disappear.

37

Close Shave

Busy fussing about the big man who'd just made an entry, none bothered about the small boy making an exit.

Mirchi sauntered out unescorted into the walled enclosure and then the large hall through which he'd come in. But this time, he noticed more than he had done before. He saw that some statues had tags; others had chalk markings. He couldn't make sense of any of them, but spotting a torn tag on the floor, he bent down pretending to scratch his toe, then slipped it quickly into his pocket.

Walking on, he noticed people kneeling by some of the sculptures. A bespectacled man with an apron was on a low stool beside the Buddha's leg, a tray of tools by his feet. At first, it appeared as though he was painting the statue, but after watching for a few minutes, Mirchi realized the man seemed to be cleaning it. Ahead, someone was polishing a brass bell, while another appeared to be filling a gaping crack on one of the ornamental pillars.

Just as he was about to step out of the magic-cave world and into the real-factory-world, he stopped, his eyes nearly popping out. The loader he'd seen outside had rolled in his trolley of cylinders along an aisle and was beside a foot-high stone idol wrapped inside layers of bubble paper. Together with his colleague, he was lifting the piece and placing it inside the hollowed-out cylinder! Mirchi's jaw dropped as he saw the idol disappear into the belly of the empty gas cylinder, where the men then fastened it securely into place. Once that was done, the top half of the cylinder was placed upon the bottom and screwed on like a lid. When the two parts fused together, it was impossible to tell that this was any different from a regular gas cylinder.

'Kal raat ka Hong Kong consignment,' the loader said to his colleague, as he scribbled a symbol on the cylinder with a marker. 'Yeh, or woh,' the man pointed to the strange idol with the cracked arm.

Dekh Munna...kya idea hai! Mirchi began chattering in his head, when it suddenly occurred to him that he had Aaji's mobile phone in his pocket. Remembering the strategy Meera had used at the police station, Mirchi whistled to catch the loader's attention, then held up his little finger.

Turning to Mirchi, the loader pointed him to a cemented block at the back.

Mirchi made a dash towards the washroom block, pretending to be in a hurry. Then turning back to check if he was being watched, he hid behind a trolley parked on the side. After looking this way and that, Mirchi extracted the phone from his pocket, then held it as close to his body as possible with trembling hands. Unlocking it quickly with the code Meera had shown him, he tapped on the camera.

CLICK. CLICK.

Two pictures of the antique articles scattered about the floor—idols, pillars, pots.

CLICK. CLICK.

Two pictures of the cylinder.

CLICK.

A close-up of the bronzes.

'Oye, Akku!' a loud voice gave him a jolt. Startled, Mirchi nearly dropped the phone. Slipping it quickly back into his pocket, he froze at the spot, his hands sweaty, his mouth dry. His eyes darted this way, then that, his heart pounding wildly within his chest. Had someone seen him? But when nothing happened for a few moments, he exhaled hard and emerged from behind the trolley. Then, he quietly slipped away.

Making his way briskly past the heavy door, then the corridor, least interested now in the soap making or marble slabs, Mirchi headed straight to the main gate of the factory. He stepped out and took a deep breath, the adrenalin rush now ebbing. Snorting happily to spot his master, Munna came running towards him, as Mirchi's eyes spotted Meera and Malhar standing behind a row of trucks. He ran towards them, never having felt so exhilarated and drained at the same time.

'I'm so glad you're safe,' said Meera. 'We were starting to get worried!'

'Did you see Mrs Shenoy's murti?' asked Malhar.

'No!' Mirchi shook his head, quivering with excitement. 'But I seeing much bigger scam.'

38

Consultation

Meera gazed at the gold disk embossed with the national emblem through a curtain of tears. *Police Medal for Gallantry*: her eyes scanned the words again and again, as she stood before the framed medal awarded to her Baba by the President some years ago. *Was it possible*, the voice inside raised its ugly head again, *was it possible that Baba knew about this Pasha uncle*? She dismissed the thought. It was too painful to even consider.

'If a consignment is leaving tomorrow night,' whispered Malhar, 'we don't have a choice, Didi, we have to tell someone!'

Meera exchanged a glance with Mirchi, then popped her head into her mother's study, 'Ma,' her voice was low. 'I need to talk to you.'

'Can this wait, Meera? I've got to finish drafting this petition,' said Madhavi Pradhan, without looking up from her laptop.

'No,' Meera stepped in. 'It's urgent.'

The tone of her voice more than her words, compelled Mrs Pradhan to turn. 'Come inside, Meera,' she sung around on her swivel chair. 'What's the matter?'

Meera looked back and nodded. Malhar walked in. Then Mirchi. Followed by Munna.

'What's going on, Meera?' Madhavi Pradhan looked on in puzzled amusement.

'We want to tell you something,' said Malhar, then closed the door behind them.

'Have you gotten yourselves into trouble? Who is this boy? And this dog? What happened?'

'This is Mirchi,' Meera introduced their partner. 'He takes the raddi because Subhash chacha has gone to his gaon. And that's Munna. They're our friends.'

'Are you okay?' Mrs Pradhan examined Mirchi from head to toe, as Munna sniffed her feet. 'Come in, sit down.'

Mirchi stood still, his expression vacant.

'Sit!' Meera tugged at Mirchi's arm, pulling him down onto a divan by the wall.

'Malhar! Have you done something? Did you hurt this boy? Or the dog?'

'Why do you always assume I've done something wrong?' Malhar threw up his hands.

'Okay then why did you shut the door?' Madhavi Pradhan rubbed the soft hair behind Munna's ear. 'What's the big secret?'

'Ma, it's a long long story.' Meera sat on the window ledge. 'Please listen to the whole story before you say anything.'

~

Madhavi Pradhan stared at the screen, gobsmacked.

'Ma, it won't zoom more than this,' said Meera, taking the camera back from her mother. 'I'm telling you. It is Pasha uncle!'

'Mirchi beta,' Mrs Pradhan finally spoke. 'You have been so brave. I can't believe what you have ...I mean... this is all so unbelievable,' she muttered in bewilderment.

Seated on the edge of the divan, Mirchi straightened up, tearing his eyes away from the enormous shelf filled with thick leather-bound legal books on the opposite wall—he'd never seen so many books in a single place—even at a raddi store! He gave an awkward nod.

'Ma!' protested Malhar. 'I have been brave too!'

'Of course, of course.' His mother ran her hand over his head. 'You all have been incredibly brave. But why... why did you do this? What if you'd gotten yourselves into trouble?'

'We had no idea, Ma,' explained Meera. 'We had no clue that searching for Mrs Shenoy's idol would unearth all this.'

'We were just trying to help her,' added Malhar, rubbing Munna who was curled up by his feet.

Madhavi Pradhan sighed. 'Such good kids.' She stood up, too shocked to say anything concrete. 'You all have your heart in the right place. I am so proud.' She began pacing up and down the room. 'But this,' she looked at the tag Mirchi had picked up from the factory floor, 'is very confusing. It says here SHALIMAR HANDICRAFTS. So perhaps what Mirchi saw behind the soap factory was some sort of handicraft manufacturing unit?'

'But why would they hide normal handicrafts inside cylinders?' argued Meera. 'Obviously that means they're doing something fishy.'

'We should talk to someone who understands what's going on. Otherwise, it's just speculation, that too, based on our half-baked understanding of the problem,' sighed their mother. 'If we're going to make such a big allegation about antique smuggling...worse, if we're going to point fingers at a top police officer, it can't be just conjecture and surmise.'

'Conjecture and surmise?' Malhar narrowed his eyes. 'Meaning?'

'Meaning guess work.' Mrs Pradhan sat back down. 'We are assuming these items that Mirchi saw are stolen. We are assuming that they're running a smuggling racket at the back of the soap factory. We are assuming Officer Naik was there for something clandestine. There is no proof. And we are deducing all this based on what a child has seen...it just won't hold up. We can't make such big accusations without something more substantial.'

'Ma, you think,' Meera hesitated, 'you think Baba knows that his friend is...'

'Not a chance in hell, Meera! How could you even think of such a thing?'

Meera exhaled hard, a wave of relief washing over her. The very thought that her father would knowingly be friends with an officer involved in something illegal had been tormenting her. Her mother's response gave her some cheer.

'Why can't we tell Baba to go and raid the place?' suggested Malhar. 'Hopefully he will also find Shenoy aunty's idol.'

'Malhar, the police can't just randomly raid a place.' His mother drummed her fingers on her desk. 'Also, this is no longer only about locating one idol. If our understanding is correct, this is a high-level smuggling racket you guys have discovered. But I'm wondering if this would come under Baba's purview at all.' She rotated her chair, leaned into her computer and began typing something. 'It looks like complaints of this nature would go to the Idol Wing of the Police.'

'Wing?' Mirchi winced, flapping his arms like a bird.

'Wing also means uh...department,' smiled Malhar.

'So it seems like the police have a special department called the Idol Wing to tackle the problem of idol theft in the state,' Madhavi Pradhan scanned the police portal. 'And...hmmm...let's see...the Idol Wing is under the charge of a Deputy Commissioner who is—' she stopped and covered her mouth with her hands.

'What?' Meera peered into the monitor.

'It's Samir Naik!' Malhar read the name displayed on screen.

For a few moments, nobody said a word. They just stared at the screen, then at each other.

'What...uh...what now?' Meera sat down beside a dozing Munna.

'Baba is travelling. He won't come back before evening, and this is too much to tell him on the phone,' mumbled Mrs Pradhan.

'But Ma, you heard what Mirchi said. Some consignment is leaving for Hong Kong tomorrow. There isn't much time!'

'I know! I know!' her mother stood up again, crossed her hands and leaned against her desk. 'Maybe we go with this to Shaaji, or Anurag,' she said, referring to SSP Pradhan's immediate deputies in Maulsari.

'Ma, do you know them well enough? Are you sure they can be trusted?' said Meera. 'I mean, what if they turn out to be like this Naik?'

Madhavi Pradhan let out a sigh. Having spent less than six months in Maulsari, she didn't know anybody in her husband's command-chain or staff too well. 'Good thinking, Meera,' she patted her daughter. 'You're right, we shouldn't complicate matters by going to the wrong people. I will speak to Baba as soon as he gets back this evening but in the meantime, I think we need more information to understand what the hell is really going on! And,' she snapped her fingers, 'I think I know just the right person to help us make sense of it all!'

39

Down the Well

'Sha...aku...nata,' Mirchi struggled with the name displayed on the wooden plate nailed to the door.

'Shakuntala Sahasrabudhe,' Meera read it for him, feet dangling restlessly on the bench outside the office of the curator of the Rajmata Stepwell and Museum. Only a few days ago they'd frowned at their mother's suggestion to visit this historic place, and yet, now here they were! She looked at her watch. Her mother and Mrs Ghosh had been inside, chatting with the curator about the entire episode for nearly an hour. And how typical of them to play that grown-up card and keep them out, even when they had been at the centre of it all!

'Aur yeh?' Mirchi pointed to a second string of letters below the first. 'Yeh kaun hai?'

'That is not another person!' guffawed Malhar, slapping his hands together. 'Those are her qualifications.'

The door opened. Ma stepped out, followed by Paromita Ghosh. The children stood at attention. Then an elderly lady dressed elegantly in a starched pink saree draped over a half-sleeved blouse came out of the room.

'You must be Mirchi?' she said, bending down slightly to bring her face to his level.

Mirchi nodded.

'It is an honour to meet you!' she smiled gently, looking at him from under her thin rimmed glasses, genuine warmth in her voice. 'I am Shakuntala, director of this beautiful monument and museum.'

Mirchi gaped at her without blinking. Not only was she a fine memsahib like Mrs Ghosh and Mrs Pradhan, but she'd just stepped out of a large office in an important-looking building and had a big name and designation. It felt like a dream!

Mrs Ghosh put her arm around Mirchi's shoulder, noticing his discomfort. 'I don't think he realizes yet—the extent of what he has unearthed.'

'And you both,' said Mrs Sahasrabudhe, turning to Malhar and Meera, 'I can't thank you enough for starting out on this adventure. You have no idea how immensely helpful you have been to us.'

The three children exchanged proud glances, faces beaming, shoulders upright, hearts swelling with pride, although they weren't quite sure how they had been of any help to the grey-haired woman.

'And you, madam,' she turned to Mrs Ghosh. 'You have made no less a contribution by offering them such excellent help and guidance.'

'It's uh...really the kids...they were Holmes...I only played Watson,' shrugged Mrs Ghosh. 'And naturally we had Byomkesh Babu's blessings!' She pointed heavenward, as if he were a divine force watching down on them.

'Shall we,' Mrs Sahasrabudhe pointed to the door at the end of the corridor. 'The visiting hours are over, so we should now have the whole place to ourselves.'

'Sure,' said Madhavi Pradhan, beckoning the kids to follow.

'Where are we going?' whispered Meera, tagging alongside her mother.

'You'll see,' replied her mother solemnly.

'Yes. We are at the stepwell,' Mrs Sahasrabudhe said into her phone as she led them all down an aisle that opened out into a compound at the end of the building. 'Please come as soon as you can. I cannot trust anyone else but you.'

'Who is she talking to?' Meera asked her mother.

'No idea,' Mrs Pradhan shrugged.

'Since this is your first time here, let me explain.' Mrs Sahasrabudhe turned into a stoned porch leading to a stairway that descended into what seemed like a pit. 'This is a well,' she began. 'Unlike other monuments you may have seen, that are palaces for the luxury of kings, or tombs for the burial of queens, this is a well to provide water—that most basic of all resources—for ordinary people, and built by a queen. That is what makes this such a unique and wonderous monument.'

The children looked around in amazement as they walked down, leaving the heat and humidity behind them with every step into the cool, refreshing interior.

'These are what we call surasundaris,' Mrs Sahasraudhe pointed to a panel of exquisitely crafted sculptures. 'Celestial maidens.'

Meera gaped at the stunning figures of women hewn on the brown stone. One gazed longingly into a mirror; while another gracefully slipped on her anklets; a third posed under the branch of a tree. It seemed so real and yet it seemed so unreal! *I really should work on that summer project*, she thought.

'What is this?' Malhar ran his fingers on an engraving in a script he had never seen before.

'It is an inscription,' replied the curator as they descended further down the steps. 'It reads: there is a special place in hell for those who waste water.'

'How insightful!' smiled Madhavi Pradhan.

'And this,' Mrs Sahasrabudhe stopped as they got to what seemed like the lowest level of the tank. 'This may look familiar to you?' She pointed out a statue to Mirchi.

Mirchi stared uncomprehendingly at her, then at the statue before him. 'Haan haan haan! I seeing!' he nodded his head vigorously. 'Factory mein!'

'It is an ardha-naareeshwara,' said Mrs Sahasrabudhe.

'Ardha kya?'

'Half Shiva, half Parvati,' she explained. 'Ardha meaning half, naree meaning female and ishwar meaning the lord. The lord in half male and half female form is called the Ardha-nareeshwara. It is one of the most difficult figures to sculpt because the male form on the right has to blend seamlessly and aesthetically into the female form on the left, and mind you the material is stone! It is the high point of Indian art!'

'Shundor!' Mrs Ghosh cupped her chin with her palms, gazing at the figure with starry eyes.

'Yes, it is stunning,' said the curator, her voice dropping. 'But,' she sighed, 'what you see before you is not the original!'

'What?' the children gasped.

'But it says here,' Meera read from a little plaque below the figure. 'That it's a tenth-century sculpture.'

'That was so, but the tenth-century piece is not this.' Mrs Sahasrabudhe pressed her eyes shut, tormented to let out the words she was about to utter, 'The original was stolen!'

'Stolen?' Another gasp.

She tapped her phone to open the photograph Mirchi had taken at the factory, sent to her by Ms Pradhan. Then she zoomed in. 'Look,' she said, 'look at the mudra—the gesture on Shiva's hand here, and look at this one.'

They all peered into the picture, then at the statue before them.

'And the mekhela—the belt across Parvati's hip—you can see it's not at the same position, it's slightly lower. And the keyuri—the armlet—it is thinner.'

All eyes turned once again to the phone, then the statue. 'So that's what my classmates names Mekhala and Keyuri really mean!' Malhar whispered to Meera.

'Oh my! The differences are so fine,' gasped Mrs Pradhan. 'But yes, now that you point it out, I do see them.'

Mrs Ghosh shook her head. 'I did not know thieves were so skilled!'

'I still can't tell the difference,' Malhar rubbed his eyes.

'If I show you a picture of Kohli,' said Mrs Sahasrabudhe, 'and tell you it's Dhoni...won't you know?'

'Arre Dhoni ko kaise Kohli samjhega?' chuckled Mirchi.

'To a trained eye,' she smiled, 'these are just as different! But yes, I must admit the artist who made the fake is incredibly talented.'

'So, wait a minute,' Meera held out a hand. 'This...this one...' she pointed to the picture Mirchi had taken, 'is the original?'

Mrs Sahasrabudhe inhaled hard then nodded with a painful sigh. 'And from the picture, it looks like the murti's hand has cracked during the theft.'

'But what happened after that?' inquired Ma. 'Don't you have a CCTV camera here?' She spun around, her eyes scanning the walls. 'Did you inform the police?'

'I did,' Mrs Sahasrabudhe nodded sombrely. 'I was on leave for a month. That's when the theft happened. Nobody even noticed till my return. The day I came back and saw it...' she pressed her eyes shut. 'It was the most shocking thing I'd ever seen! And a ruder shock awaited me. The CCTV footage had been wiped clean! There was nothing! Nothing!' her voice trembled. 'And ...now that you bring me all this information...I realize that the rudest shock of all was still to come!'

'What do you mean?' Ma stepped closer.

'Oh I just don't know what I must do, Madhavi.' The curator leaned on Mrs Pradhan and pressed her hand. 'I just don't know whom to trust anymore!'

'I can understand how distressing this must be for you,' Mrs Pradhan consoled the other woman as they heard hurried steps behind them.

'Ah! There he is,' said Mrs Sahasrabudhe, a flash of relief on her troubled face. 'The one person I trust blindly. The man for the moment! Thank you for coming so quickly after my call,' she said to a bearded man with dishevelled hair walking down the well.

'What happened?' the man approached hurriedly. 'Why the urgent phone call? Is everything alright?'

'Everyone,' Mrs Sahasrabudhe turned to the others. 'Meet the one person who can guide us through this gloom—one of the most eminent art historians of our country,' she introduced the man, as Meera stood by, stunned and frozen. 'Meet Professor Abhay Mitra!'

40

A Mess of It All!

'Oh no NO NO NO NO!' Meera covered her mouth with both hands. 'Now Mrs Sahasrabudhe is telling that Mad Eye Moody the full story!' She looked at her mother, then tugged her arm. 'Ma...'

Listening intently to the detailed briefing being given to Professor Abhay Mitra by Mrs Sahasrabudhe, and filling in the blanks in her narrative, Madhavi Pradhan paid no attention to her daughter.

'MAAAAA,' Meera repeated, the tug more forceful, the voice more agitated.

'We're talking, Meera!' Mrs Pradhan fixed Meera with an admonishing stare.

Meera exhaled hard, turned around and stomped about in a huff.

'What happened?' Malhar raised his eyebrows.

'This is the same art historian I told you about!' Meera said in a hushed tone.

'What? The same guy who wanted Mrs Shenoy's murti?'

'Yes!' Meera nodded. 'He even has some police case against him!'

'How do you know it's him?

'Don't you remember I checked him up online? I showed you a picture of that Mad Eye Moody-look-alike!'

Malhar nodded, his eyes wide with a hint of recognition. 'What if he stole the idol and sold it to Hathoda?'

'Precisely!' Meera slapped her forehead with her palm. 'And if he gets to know that Mirchi is the one who got all this information,' Meera bit her nails, 'who knows what that Hathoda will do to Mirchi after that.'

'Didi! We have to do something,' said Malhar.

'Mirchi! Run!' Meera shook Mirchi by his shoulders, her voice bubbling with tension.

'Huh?' Mirchi frowned, not having followed a word of the hurried chatter between brother and sister.

'Bhag Mirchi! Bhag jaa!' Malhar pushed his arm. 'Before that uncle sees you.'

'Kyun?' Mirchi didn't budge. 'Kaun hai yeh uncle?'

'He may be...th smu...gg...' the words dried out in Meera's throat because the devilish-looking bespectacled man had walked up to them and was standing right beside her.

'So,' he said, peering down at the children like they were antiquities in a museum, 'you are the bright young minds behind this sensational discovery, are you?'

Meera swallowed hard. *Too late to run!*

'I am delighted to meet you,' he said, his voice husky, his gaze piercing.

Heart pounding wildly, Meera was overcome by an urge to push Professor Mad-Eye Moody into the pool of water, and make a quick escape up the steps with Mirchi and Malhar. The next moment, she wanted to yell at her mother and tell her how she'd gone and jinxed the whole operation! *Grown-ups! The moment you got them involved in anything, they just take over and make a mess of it all.*

41

Misunderstood Matters

This is what Bruce from Finding Nemo *would look like, if he laughed like the hyenas from* The Lion King, thought Malhar, as he stared at Abhay Mitra sitting next to him at the table inside the director's office, laughing uncontrollably, head thrown back, hands patting knee, body jerking hysterically. 'Oh this is hilarious!'

Drawn in by the man's infectious laughter, unbeknown to him, Mirchi had begun laughing too.

Meera bit her lip, then looked nervously at her mother. *Was bringing this to her attention yet another mistake?*

'You children are smart,' Mrs Sahasrabudhe interlocked her fingers on her desk, as a peon placed glasses of water before each of them. 'But you're still children...'

'Let me explain.' Abhay Mitra pressed the tips of his thumb and index finger into the edge of his eyes, as he finally stopped laughing. 'Over the years, the powers that be have used every weapon to discredit and silence me. They've dragged me into controversies, humiliated me publicly, harmed me physically, and even filed police cases to intimidate me.'

'Because he's been the lone wolf fighting relentlessly against this idol smuggling racket,' explained Mrs Sahasrabudhe. 'Painstakingly cataloguing sculptures and antiquities, tracking down thieves and smugglers, following up with authorities across the world...'

'So, you mean,' Meera's eyes lit up. 'This police case against you for idol theft—it was not real?'

'It is real,' said Abhay Mitra. 'Some of the big names involved in this racket got together and filed a case against me. They alleged that I was stealing murtis from temples. They thought it would shut me up, stop my fight against them. But it helped them achieve nothing of that sort. It only made me more determined to fight this menace. And with no evidence to back their allegation, the police had to eventually close the case. That's the news article you saw,' he nodded at Meera.

Meera breathed a sigh of relief, and reached for a glass of water. 'I'm so sorry,' she winced, her face red with embarrassment, 'this seems to have been a terrible misunderstanding.'

'Good heavens!' Abhay Mitra shook his head. 'To think that you kids thought me to be some dangerous maniacal double-dealing smuggler!'

'So they filed a false case against you?' Madhavi Pradhan leaned in. 'It's very disturbing when people abuse due process of the law like that...'

'Their business is worth hundreds of millions of dollars, madam,' said Abhay Mitra. 'And I am an annoying spoke in their money-spinning wheel. They'd do anything to get me out of the way. Filing a false case is a pittance.'

Madhavi Pradhan turned her concerned face to the three children and swallowed hard. They'd had simply no idea that they'd been playing with fire!

Mrs Ghosh gasped, 'Hundreds of millions of dollars?'

'Wahi toh!' Abhay Mitra pulled out a dossier from his bag, 'You children just don't know what a mountain you have unearthed,' he lay it on the table and flipped it open. 'Let me explain.'

42

Hi-fi Chor

'This is Subhash Kapoor, owner of a prestigious art gallery in New York,' Abhay Mitra pointed to the photograph in his file. 'And, the most notorious of art thieves. He's been smuggling ancient idols out of our temples for decades.'

All eyes settled on the picture of the middle-aged man in the file. 'But he...' Mrs Ghosh peered at the photograph, 'He looks so...I mean...not like a smuggler at all.'

'What do you think art smugglers look like?' smiled the professor. 'Pirates with eye-patches? Bandits with big moustaches? Underworld dons with guns? Well, thieves of the art world are not like that lot. They're sophisticated scoundrels, wining and dining in high society.'

'Hi-fi chor!' chuckled Mirchi.

'Their modus operandi,' continued the professor, 'is to identify unused temples in remote areas, then hire thieves to steal idols from there. Small-time artists are employed to touch up these sculptures to give them a newish look.'

'I seeing,' Mirchi nodded. 'One kaarigar painting Buddha statue at factory....'

'Likely he wasn't painting it but removing the encrustation,' explained Abhay Mitra. 'You see, statues that have been around for hundreds of years get battered by the wind and rain. So they look old, unlike new ones that are bright and smooth. To give the old ones a modern look to fool the authorities, they remove the encrustation.'

'What a well-planned operation!' exclaimed Mrs Ghosh.

'It's a multi-pronged and well-oiled system,' said the professor. 'They get craftsmen to make replicas of these idols and mix them up in a large consignment. Add on a handicraft tag to give it a clean authentic look, and then it is shipped off to America, Hong Kong, Australia and so on, where there is a hungry market for the antiques.'

'So this tag that Mirchi brought from the site,' Madhavi Pradhan produced it from her purse, 'is just hogwash?'

'A smokescreen,' nodded the professor, 'to hoodwink the customs officials at the port, in case they check. You see, there is an international convention and a law passed in 1972 in India, under which any antiquity that is more than hundred years old cannot be taken out of the country. So if a particular statue is found to have been taken out after 1972, the recipient will have no choice but to return it. Hence they make it look like it's a new statue or alternatively that it was taken out of India before 1972.'

'This is just so mind boggling,' Mrs Ghosh held her head. 'But tell me, sir, who is paying hundreds of millions of dollars for these idols?'

'Museums, art galleries, private collectors,' shrugged Abhay Mitra. 'The famous museums of the West—they're all filled with stolen artefacts, aren't they? And how unabashedly they continue to display their colonial loot. That trend continues even today, only in less apparent ways. Collectors in the West continue to thirst for art looted from Africa and Asia. Even some big names that auction pieces for millions have traded in stolen works. Some do it without knowing, some with full knowledge that it's stolen. While they all claim to checking and doing due diligence before purchasing art works, often it is no more than mere optics and formality.'

'I am unable to understand,' Madhavi Pradhan exhaled deeply. 'How are these idols being stolen so brazenly from our temples?'

'Ma'am, with all due respect, there are over two million temples in India. Tell me, how is it possible to guard them all? And just look at their intricate set-up—

soap and granite factory for a front, gas cylinders for transport, handicraft tags as diversions—no wonder we haven't been able to track down these guys despite days of searching after the ardha-nareeshwara went missing from here.'

'Don't forget to add,' said Mrs Sahasrabudhe, 'top cops in cahoots! If those who are meant to be guardians are themselves participants in the plunder, no wonder our precious heritage is vanishing right under our noses! As I was about to tell you,' she turned to Madhavi Pradhan, 'the biggest revelation of it all for me was this.' She extracted a folder from her drawer and pulled out a sheet of paper from it. 'When I noticed the theft after returning from my leave, I immediately wrote to the officer in-charge of our Idol Wing, Mr Naik. And this,' she said putting on her reading glasses, 'is a printout of the email response I got...' She began to read.

'Dear Mrs Sahasrabudhe,

I am deeply saddened to hear about the callous regard to security at a prestigious institution like the Rajmata Stepwell and Museum. As Director, how did you allow a theft of this magnitude to happen? It shocks me to note that you are reporting this several days, perhaps weeks after it has taken place and further that there is no CCTV footage. It would have been of huge help in the investigation.

Anyway, thank you for alerting us. You can be assured we will do our best to take action. Please send us photographs and every detail that you may have about the concerned idol—the original and the duplicate to aid our enquiries.

In the meantime, I request you not to inform anybody in the media or the local police about this theft, as not only will this bring bad publicity and disrepute to the museum, your good self and to our department, but I have every reason to believe that some local police officers in Maulsari may be compromised and working for the smugglers.

Please communicate strictly only with me.

Regards,

Samir Naik'

Mrs Sahasrabudhe sat back with a sigh. 'Now I know why I was being asked to communicate only directly with him. And why nothing at all has happened for months!'

'Oh the cheek of this man!' Madhavi Pradhan fumed. 'He has the audacity to say the local police is compromised when he is involved neck deep in this!'

'Mr Naik even visited the museum two days ago. He took pictures, asked questions, examined our staff, I thought he's come all the way to investigate the case, that he seemed genuinely concerned,' she exhaled hard.

'The irony is,' Abhay Mitra shook his head, 'he's probably here in Maulsari to provide safe passage to the ardha-nareeshwara out of the country.'

'What do we do now, Abhay?' asked Mrs Sahasrabudhe. 'Only you can guide us.'

'Mrs Pradhan,' reflected the bespectacled professor thoughtfully, 'as you rightly said, you did not have enough substance to go to the police earlier. And you did the right thing by coming here. But now we have clear evidence of a stolen sculpture in the factory. There's enough to tip off the police.'

'But going to the Idol Wing is pointless,' said Mrs Sahasrabudhe. 'How do we know if this Naik's deputies are not in on this too?'

'No, not the Idol Wing. We will have to bypass them,' said the professor. 'Ma'am, when will SSP Pradhan be back in Maulsari?'

'I have been in constant touch with him,' Madhavi Pradhan looked into her phone. 'He is on his way back and will be at the office within the next hour.'

'Good,' nodded Abhay Mitra. 'When you meet him, please give him the full background, so he leads the operation himself and takes along only his most trusted officers to execute the raid. We don't want the information leaking or give them a chance to escape.'

'A raid?' Malhar's eyes twinkled with excitement, as Meera pulled out her diary.

'Given the consignment leaves tomorrow,' said Abhay Mitra, 'there's no other choice. We have to act tonight.'

Looking down at the page in her diary, Meera added yet another line to her list of titles.

Case of the Stolen Jewellery
Case of the Missing Idol
Case of the Vanishing Gods

'And yes,' added the professor warily. 'No speaking about this to anybody at all. Because these days,' his eyes darted this way and that, 'even the walls have ears!'

43

Raid

'This is so unfair!' Malhar kicked the sofa. 'Just sitting here and waiting like we're nobodies.'

'Beta, for the umpteenth time,' his mother exhaled hard, 'It's not a picnic!'

'But…*we* did all the work! *We* figured out everything! Baba could have given us special permission if he wanted.'

'Special permission? To send children on a police raid into a smuggler's den? Have you lost your mind, Malhar?'

Malhar stomped about the room and plonked himself by the window ledge. A nightjar called from a tree outside as cicadas kept up their croaking chorus.

Madhavi Pradhan's mobile buzzed. 'It's Baba,' she said, her lips curving instantly into a smile. She read the message: 'Raid successful. Recovered huge quantities of stolen antiquities. Turn on the news. Love to my M&M. Tell them Baba is proud of them. Won't be back until morning. Don't wait up for me.'

'Aaji! They did it!' Meera sat up on the sofa, put aside her book and picked up the TV remote. 'Come!'

'Yes! Yes! Yes!' Malhar punched his fists in the air.

Aaji appeared from her bedroom, rubbing her sleepy eyes with her knuckles, then plonked herself on the couch and reached out for her glasses. 'Ganpati Bappa,' she brought her hands together.

'Morya!' roared Malhar.

'Breaking News! Burning News!' a yelling anchor appeared on the television, behind a screen of graphic flames. 'Ladies and gentlemen, tonight we bring you the biggest news of the year! Police in the little coastal town of Maulsari bust a HUGE, a MASSIVE, an ENORMOUS, a GIGANTIC, idol smuggling racket. And tonight, only on our channel, we're asking the big question—'

Grabbing the remote from his sister's hand, Malhar switched the channel.

'We bring you the news before anybody else,' an animated anchor paced up and down the studio like a show pony, as devotional music played in the background with tacky graphics of idols whooshing across the screen like jet planes.

'God help us,' Madhavi Pradhan took the remote from Malhar and switched.

'Aaj ki khaas khabar,' an anchor screamed, as a theatrical troupe performed a Ramlila-like act in the studio behind him. A small rectangle on the top corner showed visuals from the raid. 'There's Baba!' Malhar jumped, as they all leaned forward to take a closer look. The SSP was pointing to a row of objects—terracotta figures and bronze statues, copper coins and ancient scrolls—placed on a white cloth-covered table, a dozen officers standing by his side, their faces lit up by bursts of flash.

'And that's Shahji uncle,' Meera scrunched her eyes and moved closer, to spot her father's deputy in the inset box, speaking into a cluster of microphones.

'Why have they muted them?' Madhavi Pradhan tutted, as the audio-feed stayed on the screaming faces in the main part of the screen—jobless lawyers and out-of-work film stars, self-proclaimed godmen and self-styled pundits—experts on all matters under the sun, battling it out in a closely contested screaming match. With a sigh, she tapped the remote.

Another channel, same story. Lady dressed in shimmering blue saree alongside ten screaming heads, delivered her rehearsed lines, trying to whip up an emotional frenzy, swaying her round head from side to side. 'First the invaders, then the colonial powers, destroyed and looted India's ancient antiquities for hundreds of years,' she lamented, feigning deep anguish and sorrow. 'And it pains me immensely to say this, but today, unfortunately, Indians have taken that task upon themselves! And now exclusively on our channel, an interview with the whistleblower who exposed this ugly saga.'

‘Put off this turnip-faced drama queen,’ Aaji muttered. ‘And who is that stuffed capsicum?’ she peered at the rotund man on screen who was speaking about the raid like he’d pulled it all off himself. ‘Is he that Mitra fellow you told me about?’

‘No no!’ Meera’s jaw dropped. ‘What do they mean he’s the whistleblower?’

‘We are the whistleblowers, you TURNIP FACE!’ Malhar crawled to the television screen, scowling menacingly before the news anchor.

‘Ma,’ Meera turned to her mother in disdain. ‘Who is this strange man? We don’t even know who he is.’

‘At least now you know how news shows are made,’ Madhavi reached for the TV remote and this time, she shut it off. ‘Not worth our time,’ she sat back as the screen went blank, and both silence and sanity were restored.

‘I watch all these crime shows on TV,’ said Aaji, rising to go to the kitchen. ‘I didn’t realize I had two detectives in my own house! But tell me, why are they not mentioning the children?’

‘I spoke to Dhananjaya about this,’ said their mother. ‘We decided it is important to protect their identities. We don’t want the smugglers to know it was them. Mirchi will be in trouble if Hathoda and his lot find out he was involved. So although Malhar is disappointed to have the spotlight snatched away, I’m afraid it must be done!’

'Tarhee!' Aaji slapped the back of her right hand with the palm of the left as she ambled into the kitchen. 'That is why the field is open for these jokers to jump in and grab the limelight.'

'Beta, in all the commotion of the day, I forgot to tell you,' Madhavi Pradhan turned to Meera, 'today that NGO client of mine informed me that they managed to arrange a hearing aid for Sarla's daughter. The little girl actually heard a sound for the first time today! Because of you,' she squeezed Meera's arm.

'Really?' Meera squealed, feeling a rush of goosebumps on her arm.

'Such good children,' Aaji returned from the kitchen with a plate containing rice grains, mustard seeds and some salt. 'Don't want anyone casting an evil eye on my sona bacchas,' she said, motioning for them to line up before her. 'These days nobody can be trusted,' she repeated her usual refrain. 'Even those we count as well-wishers sometimes become back-stabbers. Yesterday, in *Crime Watch*, they showed a son cheating his parents...can you imagine?'

'Arre hey kaay, Aaji,' Meera protested, obeying reluctantly. 'What has that got to do with us? And what is all this nazar business?'

'Alya gelyachi, gharachi baharchi, konachi drust lagle asel, tar jau de...' Aaji muttered, circling the plate around the children, before pottering back to the kitchen to burn all the ingredients over a fire.

Reaching out for her blue diary on the table, Meera opened to the first page.

Mystery of the Stolen Jewellery -

Mystery of the Missing Idol-

Mystery of the Vanishing Gods - √

She placed a tick mark on the last row, then sat back. Yes, this did seem like a watershed moment—they'd unearthed a massive scam and stopped items of national heritage from leaving the country's shores just in time. But they weren't quite there yet, she thought, tapping the pencil on the page, as Aaji smeared ash on their foreheads. One done. Two to go!

44

A Pat and a Warning

Face scrubbed, hair combed, dressed in a bright yellow shirt and blue jeans, Mirchi gazed at the large dome above him at the centre of the imposing stone building, as he made his way up the wide stairway, staying close on Meera and Malhar's heels. An officer trotting down the steps stopped as he passed them, then shook hands with each of them.

'The Assistant District Superintendent,' Meera nudged Mirchi, 'Shaaji uncle, who led the raid last night.'

Eyes fixed on the many epaulets shining on the officer's uniform, Mirchi barely heard his words. 'You deserve a medal of honour,' the man was saying to them.

The children smiled, exchanged pleasantries, and walked on to the first floor, where they stopped again outside a glass door labelled, Police Control Room. Inside, phone lines buzzed, men and women in uniforms spoke frantically into their handsets, lights of various colours blinked on a dozen consoles.

'Oh you're here already.' A smiling middle-aged man walked up to them from the far end of the corridor. 'Come along this way.'

'Hello, Vijay uncle,' Meera and Malhar greeted their father's personal assistant. 'This is our friend Mirchi.'

'Please be seated,' Vijay ushered them into a carpeted waiting room outside the SSP's cabin. 'I'll let you know as soon as sir is free.'

The children shuffled in. Vijay disappeared behind the door.

'I can hear voices,' Malhar whispered, pinning his ears to the wooden partition behind a sofa. 'It's Baba.'

Meera moved closer. Mirchi continued to gaze in astonishment at everything—the high ceilings above, the soft carpet below, the national flag at one end, the framed photos of Gandhi, Nehru and Ambedkar on the wooden panels.

'This is very disturbing, Shevre,' SSP Pradhan could be heard from the other side. 'You arrested the plumber without any basis at all?'

'Sir, he...the watchman said he...' Shevre was muttering, 'was the only outsider who'd gone in that afternoon. So I thought...'

'So? That was enough to conclude he's the thief?' barked SSP Pradhan. 'Is there no difference between a police officer conducting an enquiry and the jobless neighbourhood uncle jumping to conclusions based on chit-chat? And why didn't you produce him before the magistrate? For over two weeks?'

'Sir, as you know the Devi yatra is on in full swing. I was busy with the bandobast facilities.'

'Who is this Inspector Yadav? I hear he hung the plumber boy by a rod and beat him up severely?'

'Kamlesh Yadav...uh...he is a sub-inspector at my police station, sir.'

'What does he think he's doing?'

'Sorry, sir...he...uh...we...'

'I'm ordering an enquiry. Till then this Yadav stands suspended. I shall not tolerate any third-degree measures in any police station within my jurisdiction! Is that clear?'

Seldom, if ever, had Malhar and Meera heard their father yell. It sent a chill down their spine.

'As for you, this time I will leave you with a warning,' said the SSP firmly. 'But the next time I receive a complaint about anybody at your station, I shall institute a departmental enquiry. You are responsible for the culture you foster there.'

'Thank you, sir...I mean sorry, sir.'

'You may go now!'

'Jai Hind, sir!'

A clicking of boots, followed by quick steps, and the children scurried to the sofa, picked up newspapers lying on the low table and covered their faces. The door swung open and Shevre stepped out and made a brisk exit.

'Serves him right,' Malhar grunted, as Vijay popped his head back in to say, 'You may go in now.'

Meera stood up, then knocked on the door.

'Come in,' she heard her father's deep voice.

Nodding at the others, she pushed open the door and stepped in, followed by Malhar. Mirchi stood at the door, gawking at the SSP's cabin that had opened out like a magical arena before him. The room seemed large enough to play a cricket match!

'Ah, you're here!' SSP Pradhan looked up from his desk and walked over to welcome the children. 'Won't you come in to meet Dhurandhar Bhatawdekar?' he winked at Mirchi at the door.

Mirchi smiled sheepishly at the nameplate, then stepped inside.

'Before anything else, you have the sincerest gratitude of the police department and the nation,' he said as they sat down at an enormous teak desk. 'I am just bowled over!'

The children smiled, chin up, shoulders straight.

'Now while you may think solving crimes and chasing criminals is an awful lot of fun, believe me, it can be dangerous! I am glad none of you have been harmed but don't go around believing this is how it's done. I don't want you to attempt such a thing ever again. Is that clear?'

The children exchanged glances, then nodded slightly.

'And Mirchi,' the SSP leaned forward on the desk, 'I've spent a better part of this morning hearing all about your adventure from my children. For the last few days I've been wondering how Malhar's vocabulary was suddenly filled with words like thakela and marela,' he smiled. 'Now the puzzle piece has fit!'

Mirchi scratched his head and once again flashed an awkward smile.

'Baba,' Meera reached for biscuits on a tray at the table, handed one to Mirchi, then bit into another. 'Did you find Mrs Shenoy's idol?'

'That is why I have called you here,' the SSP pushed back his chair then led them to the back door of his cabin. 'Come with me.'

'And...uh...what about Samir Naik of the Idol Wing...' asked Meera hesitantly as they followed the SSP into a brightly lit room.

'He...uh...' the SSP sighed, 'has been suspended and an enquiry has been instituted against him. Well...here we are,' he said pointing to a large table in the centre of the room filled with terracotta, stone and bronze idols, copper and gold coins, and an array of other items. A few uniformed officers were milling about; one was entering something into a laptop, another was taking photographs. They all stopped, turned and saluted the SSP.

'Please continue with your work,' said SSP Pradhan, then whispered to the children. 'This is only part of the material seized, and does not include the stone figures which were too heavy to bring in here.' He walked over to the far end of the table. 'And this,' he pointed to a little brass idol, 'is how the whole saga began!'

'You got Aunty's idol back, Baba!' Meera squealed, clutching her father's arm.

'Can we take it back and give it to her?' asked Malhar.

'It's not so simple, beta,' smiled the SSP. 'The matter will go to court where a seizure report enlisting all the items seized from the factory will be drawn up and filed. Those claiming that any of these items belong to them will have to prove it. It's a long drawn-out process. But ultimately, yes, Mrs Shenoy will get it back though it will take time.'

Mirchi gawked at the seized items, amazed at how only yesterday they'd all been at the warehouse behind the soap factory. 'And soap factory people?' he asked, his thoughts going to Hathoda and his cronies. 'Now they in jail?

'That is also a long process,' sighed the SSP. 'They will be charged for various offences like theft, house-breaking, breaking temple locks, criminal trespass...big list. And the proceedings will chug along slowly. For now, they have been arrested and are being questioned.'

'But Baba,' interjected Malhar. 'Who stole Mrs Shenoy's idol?'

'We don't know that yet,' said SSP Pradhan. 'But we have a big team working on this now, and Professor Abhay Mitra is helping trace the source of each idol. Hopefully, that will give us more leads to track down the thief in each case.'

'Sir,' Vijay appeared hurriedly by his elbow, 'Call from the CMO for you.'

SSP Pradhan nodded. 'Children, it's a busy day for us today. I've got to go. Take a quick look around, don't touch anything and I'll see you later.' He patted them all, then vanished through the door.

As Malhar and Mirchi walked around the table, taking a closer look at each piece, Meera had her eyes fixed on the police emblem embossed on a panel behind the table: *Satyameva Jayate. In truth alone is victory*. Pulling out her diary and pencil from her backpack, she opened once again to the first page.

Mystery of the Stolen Jewellery -
Mystery of the Missing Idol- √
Mystery of the Vanishing Gods - √

She placed another tick mark and exhaled in quiet satisfaction, turning her eyes again to the Mahalsa Devi. After days, Mrs Shenoy could finally have a good night's sleep!

45

An Interrupted Celebration

The celebration out on the balcony was small, but hearts and stomachs were bursting with fullness. Canvas and crayons cast aside, the table had a spread of snacks, a sprinkling of sweets and was a mine of incessant chatter. Soft music played on a stereo inside, a refreshing breeze caressed their faces, and the dazzling gulmohurs showered them intermittently with their flamboyant petals, playing silent spectators to their joy.

'This is Apu's,' Paromita Ghosh emerged from her bedroom, wiping a blue school bag with the pallu of her saree and holding it before Mirchi. 'It's just sitting in there, collecting dust.'

Wiping samosa crumbs off his mouth, Mirchi stared at the bag, then at her.

'It's for you,' she thrust the bag forward. 'And tomorrow, you will come shopping with me. We're going to get you some clean clothes, books and stationery.'

Mirchi ran his hands over the glossy Avengers sticker on the bag, then zipped it open and close. A *bag with zips that worked!* He smiled.

'Thrice a week, you will come here for lessons...to make up for all the time you've been out of school,' Mrs Ghosh sat down on the granite ledge. 'You cannot be twelve and be struggling to read.'

Mirchi bobbed his head from side to side, jostling with mixed feelings. *Of what use was reading and writing to a bhangi boy?* The nasty questions, the insulting remarks—they surfaced for a moment, then ebbed like a wave. He said nothing.

'What do you guys think about the jewels?' Meera bit into her third piece of kheer kadam. 'You think we'll find them? And the thief?'

'Arre chhodo!' Mirchi sat back, with a dismissive wave of his hands. 'We finding murti, that is a badi baat! Fawda bola na, jewellery will not be found.'

'Shhh...' Paromita Ghosh placed a finger on her lip, peeping out of the balustrade. 'That's Harsh's house on the third floor,' she whispered, pointing to a window perpendicularly below the balcony. 'Don't say such things, they'll feel bad if they hear, it'll dash their hopes.'

Meera stood up and peeped out. She could see part of Harsh Shenoy's house—Aditya's toys in a corner, a treadmill and cross-trainer near the window. 'I don't know,' she said in a hushed voice. 'I feel...I feel like we haven't completely solved the mystery yet. The last piece of the puzzle is still missing.' She flipped open her blue diary that had become a constant companion.

Thief:

1. Had the keys because there was no forcible break-in.
2. Knew that the Shenoys had a lot of jewellery in the house that day.
3. Was clever enough not to leave fingerprints.
4. Watchman Badal Singh says no outsider entered the building that afternoon.
5. Had the means (opportunity)
6. Had a motive (reason)

'It can't be some unknown person because they didn't have the keys. Who could it be...' She chewed her pencil.

'Look, I checking after you saying me to check Ali bhai— '

'Arre baba!' Mrs Ghosh narrowed her eyebrows. 'Who is this Ali bhai, now?'

'He means alibi,' smiled Meera.

'Arre haan, same-to-same!' Mirchi smacked Malhar's palm. 'After taking Chilbil from school Sarla going home, then water pump—her water turn is at 4 o'clock.'

'Water turn?' Malhar reached out for the kokam sharbat.

'We no getting water like you in house,' Mirchi explained. 'We getting in one tap for full basti. So we all taking turns to fill. Everyone having fixed time. My mother turn 4.30 in the morning.'

'Aila!' Malhar guzzled down his mango juice. 'What if she doesn't wake up one day?'

'Then no paani-vaani full day,' replied Mirchi matter-of-factly.

'Okay, so what about Sarla's water turn?' asked Meera.

'My aunt, she having big fight with Sarla that day near the water pump because Sarla breaking queue. So I knowing whole day Sarla there only in Anand Nagar. Not in Customs Colony doing chori. Ali bhai confirm! Aur yeh dekho,' he looked up with a smile. 'We finding one murti. Now other murti coming back!'

'So, big party going on.' Mr Murthi ambled into the balcony. 'I heard all about it from Paro last night and saw it on the news. You guys are terrific! I better take your autographs now before you become famous.'

'Uncle, whether you solved the scam in your bank or not,' Malhar bit into a kachori, 'we have solved our mystery!'

'Not fully,' grunted Meera, as Mrs Ghosh's phone began to buzz.

'It's Professor Abhay Mitra,' Paromita Ghosh examined the display, then tapped it on. 'Hello Obhoy moshai.

Kemon aachen?' she greeted him enthusiastically, then put the phone on speaker.

'What is he saying?' whispered Malhar, understanding nothing of the Bengali banter.

'Yes, yes, the children are very much here,' Paromita Ghosh switched languages.

'Hari Jewellers?' she nudged Meera to note it down. 'Shaheed Bhagat Singh Road. Now?' She stood up in alarm, looking at her watch.

The children exchanged glances, then shrugged.

'Acha…theek ache…theek ache…' she nodded, gesturing for them to get up immediately as she hung up the call. 'We have to go,' she said to her husband, then packed some snacks into a box and handed it to Mirchi. 'For your sister, take it home. Come now…'

'Where are we going?' Malhar rose from the table, his mouth stuffed with rasgullas.

'He said he has something,' Mrs Ghosh grabbed her purse and keys, then shepherded them out through the door, 'that might help us find the thief!'

46

Edging Closer

'You children have been such a godsend for me in my mission to track down idol thieves,' Abhay Mitra greeted them on the footpath outside Hari Jewellers, 'that I thought I owe you this!'

'What happened?' Paromita Ghosh paid the autorickshaw-wala hurriedly.

'Come,' he pushed open the shop door, leading them past a watchman, into a plush air-conditioned jewellery store with sparkling tiles and dazzling lights.

'Last night after the raid, we were at the warehouse and then at the police headquarters for hours. In fact I still haven't gone home,' he said, as they walked into a wide shop floor. 'Your father may have told you. We have been busy trying to identify, sort, and label all the smuggled goods.'

Meera nodded as they followed behind him, noticing that the professor was in the same clothes as yesterday, only the circles under his eyes were darker, and his hair more dishevelled. No wonder he looked like a freak, she thought, working himself out like a maniac.

'Come,' he led them past glass counters glittering with diamond-studded rings and ruby-encrusted earrings.

'When I noticed the pancha-loha Mahalsa Devi amongst the raided idols,' continued Professor Abhay, 'I thought of you children and poor Mrs Shenoy, and decided to begin the investigation by tracking down the trail for the murti. That led me to this jewellery store.'

'But...but...how did the murti land up here? And then how did it get to the soap factory from here?' asked Paromita Ghosh as they walked past customers inspecting gold bangles on low cushioned stools, and got to a door at the back of the store which was marked ONLY FOR STAFF.

Pressing down the handle, Abhay Mitra stepped inside. 'From here to the smugglers—through an agent who scours jewellery stores looking for antiques to supply them. As far as how it got here in the first place—that's the question I'm hoping one of you can answer. Come in,' he held the door open for the others.

They stepped gingerly inside the small room. The yellow lights of the shop had been replaced by white tube lights, and drab office desks took the place of glistening glass counters. A couple of staff were at their tables by the wall, working on computer screens, as a constable dozed off on a stool in a corner. They all stood up, then stepped aside for the professor and the string of people following him. A flurry of activity followed with the pulling and re-arranging of chairs and stools. 'So,' Abhay Mitra gestured for them to take a seat in front of one of the monitors. 'We started questioning the men who'd been arrested at the warehouse and after a lot of grilling, we found out that the Mahalsa Devi had been obtained from this jewellery store,' he said, nudging the staff member at the desk.

The technician clicked on his mouse then began scrolling through a list of items on the screen.

'And then, when I came here with the police this afternoon to enquire, we found that we were in luck! They have a functioning CCTV camera here and in fact were able to trace down footage of the day they acquired that idol.'

'Really?' Meera squealed, excited by the prospect of laying her hands on the missing piece of the puzzle.

'Because you have led us this far, and I know you were keen to solve the case, I requested the police for permission to bring you in first, before anybody else, to see if you can identify the person you are about to see,' he nodded, peering at the screen from under his glasses.

A bespectacled old man in a white safari suit entered the room, a balding man in a blue shirt following behind him. 'This is Harilal, the owner of the shop,' Abhay Mitra introduced the older of the two men. 'He had no idea the jewels and idol they bought that day were stolen. And this is Shanti Bhushan, the store manager, who actually purchased the items.' The door opened again and ASI Sakhi walked in. 'Oh!' she looked at the children in surprise.

'You know them?' asked Professor Mitra.

'Yes,' Meera smiled, glad it was Sakhi and not Inspector Shevre. 'We have met.'

They nodded at each other, then moved about the chairs to accommodate them all, as the technician tapped on a date from the list on his screen, then scrolled down to select the time. A window popped open, showing the screen divided into four sections, each displaying footage from various CCTV cameras in the store. The time stamp on the bottom corner ticked away like seconds on a digital clock.

'The police will be calling the Shenoys to find out if they can identify the man but you deserve the honour to go first. I know you have a list of suspects and perhaps one of you may identify the man.'

Ah, so it was a man! Meera could feel her pulse racing as the footage began to roll. It had to be someone who had the house key. Someone who knew the jewels were in the house. Someone with both motive and means. Who was it going to be?

47

Revelation!

'Hain?' Malhar stared at the screen.

'Ei ki?' Mrs Ghosh adjusted her glasses.

Mirchi tilted his head this way and that.

Meera drew her stool closer.

'This old man,' Shanti Bhushan pointed to the screen. 'He sold us the idol and jewels. The description of all the items he brought in to sell matches perfectly with the items stolen from the Shenoys as per the FIR filed with the police.'

'I have no idea who he is!' Malhar blinked, staring at the old man with flowing white hair as he appeared on the first screen displaying footage from the main door. He walked in alone, limping slightly with slow, laboured steps, pulling a black trolley bag with one hand, leaning on a walking stick with the other.

'Looks like he must be about sixty-five or seventy,' Professor Mitra ventured a guess.

Then the aged man appeared on the next quarter of the screen that showed footage from the camera inside the shop. He walked over to one of the sales girls, who directed him to a person further inside.

Next, he was seen on the third quarter of the screen that was displaying visuals from another location inside the shop. He sat down with some difficulty on one of the low cushions, then was seen speaking to a staff member as he adjusted his thick-rimmed spectacles over his nose. In a few moments, Mr Shanti Bhushan appeared behind the counter and could be seen speaking to the old man. After a brief exchange, a young assistant appeared by the old man's side, helping him to lift his trolley bag and place it on the counter. Then, unzipping the bag slowly, the old man extracted the first item.

'That's the same idol we saw at Baba's office this morning!' exclaimed Malhar.

'Indeed,' nodded the professor. 'Any of you know this man?'

'No,' Mrs Ghosh grimaced, as she watched some other items of jewellery emerge onto the counter.

'Na,' Mirchi shook his head, 'I collecting kachra in this mohalla so many years sahib, I knowing many peoples. But I never seeing this budhau.'

'He said they belonged to his family,' rued Mr Shanti Bhushan, 'that his wife had passed away, that he was now alone and old and didn't want the responsibility of looking after such costly items anymore. That his children were abroad and not interested in these things and so he wanted to sell them. It all sounded so genuine!' He slapped his forehead thrice. 'He even had bills and receipts for some of the items! How was I to know he was a fraud?'

'Who would doubt a senior citizen like him,' sighed Harilal. 'After all, he looked so respectable and dignified.'

Meera's eyes widened. 'Wait!' she held up her hand, then froze, thoughts running through her mind. The combination of those words felt like a key clicking into a lock.

'You know him?' Abhay Mitra turned to face her.

'I...uh...don't know...' mumbled Meera, feeling uneasy. 'Could you zoom in to the face a bit, please?' she requested the technician.

The man at the monitor clicked the mouse. The face grew larger, but was heavily pixelated and blurry.

'This doesn't help,' Meera clicked her teeth, then began biting her nails.

'The footage is nearly an hour,' said the technician. 'You want to see it all?'

'Yes,' nodded ASI Sakhi. 'Let it play.'

'This budhau not sitting still,' noted Mirchi. 'Look his legs...'

'Very fidgety,' nodded Mrs Ghosh. 'His legs are constantly jingling. Skittish fellow...it is a sign of nervousness.'

'I told him I need to examine the items more closely and call our valuer to see it,' said Mr Shanti Bhushan to explain why he was seen walking away, leaving the old man alone at the counter. 'He said he would wait but asked me to hurry up.'

'Now the old man just waits for nearly half an hour,' said the technician. 'Shall I fast forward this?'

'No!' repeated the ASI emphatically. 'Just let it play.'

They watched the old man wait, first drumming his fingers for a while on the glass counter, then rising slowly. He began pacing up and down the room, one arm behind his back, the other leaning on the stick.

'Isn't he walking differently now?' said Malhar, after watching the footage for a few minutes. 'When he entered the shop, he had a limp on his left side, now he's limping on the right.'

'Fantastic observation,' Sakhi patted the boy. 'Just play the earlier footage again,' she instructed the technician.

Malhar straightened his shoulders as the two clips were played side by side. It established beyond any doubt that the gait of the man had changed. 'Practice helps,' he chuckled; following in Fatty's footsteps surely had its benefits.

'So then he isn't an old man,' said Mrs Ghosh. 'This is a disguise.'

'It's surely a very good disguise,' said ASI Sakhi.

As the man sat down again, and placed his hands on the glass counter, Meera let out a gasp.

'What?' the professor turned to her again. 'You know him?

'I...uh...I ...don't...don't know...' Meera mumbled.

'You don't know him?' Abhay Mitra raised an eyebrow. 'Or you don't know if you know him?'

Meera covered her mouth with her hands, her head spinning, stomach churning.

'What's the matter, Meera?' asked Mrs Ghosh, noting the colour drain from the girl's face.

'I...I don't know... I don't know...' Meera exhaled hard, looking around the room. She didn't feel confident to reveal her thoughts. *Was there no window here*? It felt stifling. She stood under the draft of the air conditioner and took short breaths. 'Did he...' she turned to Shanti Bhushan, her face flushed and red, 'did the man...did he...have a strong musky perfume?'

'Uh...' Shanti Bhushan pursed his lips, 'it's been a few weeks...it's hard to say.' He scratched his head.

Meera stomped about the room, her hand on her head. 'Can you zoom into the hands please?' she returned to the technician, as everyone stared at the girl in puzzlement.

The technician clicked the mouse a few times, the man's arm, then wrist, then fingers came into view. The image was slightly blurred, but enough for Meera to miss a heartbeat.

Sometimes, the truth lays concealed behind layers of deceit. Sometimes, it stays hidden in plain sight. But rarely does it stay buried forever.

'The rings...and the watch,' Meera flopped back on her chair, then turned her pale face to Malhar. 'The watch!' she sighed. 'Do you not recognize the Rolex watch?'

48

Final Piece of the Puzzle

For a few seconds, the buzzing of the air conditioner was the only sound in the dingy room as all eyes turned from the shocked siblings to the zoomed-in images on screen. And then, a volley of questions was let loose.

'Who is this?'

'You recognize the watch?

'What are you talking about?'

'You know this man?'

'Kaun hai yeh?'

Malhar stood motionless, too shocked to say a word. Meera flipped open her diary and considered her parameters yet again, but this time against a name that had never crossed her mind as a suspect. Surprisingly, nearly everything seemed to match!

Thief:

1. Had the keys because there was no forcible break-in. - √
2. Knew that the Shenoys had a lot of jewellery in the house that day. - √

3. Was clever enough not to leave finger-prints. - √
4. Watchman Badal Singh says no outsider entered the building that afternoon. - √
5. Had the means (opportunity). - √
6. Had a motive (reason) -

Ticking off nearly every item now, Meera sat back. *What about motive? Why would Harsh Shenoy steal from his own parents?* Tapping her pencil on her diary, she recalled something. *In a proper investigation, one's theories must be based on facts; not facts on theories.* Suddenly, that line didn't seem like a riddle anymore. 'Murthi uncle!' she snapped her fingers.

'O bhogoban!' Mrs Ghosh missed a breath. 'What's Murthi got to do with all this?' she asked worriedly, her face ashen.

'He...he had said...Harsh was having money trouble... his business was down after COVID...remember?'

Paromita Ghosh let out a sigh of relief.

'Who are you talking about? Harsh Shenoy?' ASI Sakhi turned her puzzled eyes to the old man on the screen again. 'You mean their son?' she gasped.

Meera nodded. 'Wait, wait, Murthi uncle had said something else,' she turned the pages of her diary, 'about Harsh visiting him at the bank some days ago to...uh...to...adjust his home loan or something like that.'

'What a meticulous child you are!' Abhay Mitra peered into the diary. 'If only more academicians were as thorough in their research as you.'

'What happens,' said Meera, 'if someone doesn't repay their home loan?'

'The bank can take their house away,' replied Mr Shanti Bhushan matter-of-factly.

'What?' Malhar's mouth fell open. 'They'll just take away your house?'

'Let me explain,' Professor Abhay Mitra shifted his chair forward, starting off with his usual refrain. 'When you take a loan from a bank, the bank will ask you to provide some security. Meaning, you pledge something—like your house, your land, your wealth. It's called a mortgage. If you are not able to repay the loan, the bank will recover its dues by selling the property you have mortgaged.'

'So if you don't repay the loan instalment,' said Mrs Ghosh, 'the bank will first send you a reminder, then if you default again, they'll send you a warning, and if you don't repay thrice in a row, they can sell the house and recover the money!'

Eyes dropping to her diary, Meera placed a tick across the last item on her list. There it was—the final piece of the puzzle—motive. 'Yes,' she said confidently, no longer wavering and mumbling. 'I know who it is!'

49

Recalibration

'How is it possible?' Malhar scratched his head as they emerged from the store. 'How can he steal from his parents?'

'And *why* would he do it?' Mrs Ghosh hailed a passing rickshaw that drove off without heed. 'I cannot accept this...I mean Harsh is so...such a lovely person...such a good son...'

'*Never rule out those that seem unlikely. The more unlikely the suspect, the more you ought to suspect them.*' Meera thrust her diary before her art teacher. 'You had said this, remember?'

Mrs Ghosh sighed, fanning her face with the pallu of her saree. 'Let's go home and give it some thought over some cool buttermilk. The heat is making us hallucinate.'

A rickshaw slowed down by their side. They shuffled in.

'When we met Mrs Shenoy at the temple...' said Meera, as Malhar adjusted himself on her lap, 'she told us that Harsh had advised her not to put the jewels in the locker because of her weak knees. But *he*...*he* said the opposite when he met Baba.'

'Tch!' Malhar slouched, 'That could have been a slip na, Didi!'

'Yes,' agreed Mrs Ghosh, 'maybe the old woman remembered it wrongly. After all, they were so stressed at that time. It could just be an inconsequential slip.'

'No!' Meera shook her head. 'You remember you told us what Byomkesh Bakshi used to say? That everyone has a weakness...look out for it...that the culprit is bound to make a mistake?'

'Haan...so?'

'That was it! I just didn't realize then. But *that* was his big mistake. To cover up his weakness—'

'What are you talking about, Didi?' Malhar tried turning about. 'What would Gilderoy Lockhart gain by lying about this?'

'A clean image before the SSP,' said Meera, the cobwebs in her mind clearing rapidly now. 'Isn't a certificate of complete innocence something a guilty person would eagerly want? Especially someone who is seen as respectable, loved by everyone around him? This would be like a shield to...uh...to divert any chance of suspicion, to protect his reputation.'

'Meera, you need to stop reading crime stories,' said Mrs Ghosh, sitting sandwiched in the middle seat. 'Your mind is spinning out of control! What you are suggesting is just impossible. Harsh Shenoy is a decent fellow. Not some scoundrel or thief!'

'Remember those idol thieves and smugglers Professor Abhay Mitra showed us in his file?' argued Meera. 'Didn't they look all posh and sophisticated? But see what they turned out to be! Check!' she huffed. 'Check his watch and rings. I can bet they will match.'

'He isn't the only person in town wearing a Rolex watch, Meera,' Mrs Ghosh clutched the handle bar before her, as the rickshaw sped along. 'How can we just accuse someone based on that? It's a good thing we asked ASI Sakhi to wait and not take this as confirmed. We need more than just a matching watch before making such a huge accusation that can ruin someone's reputation.'

'My Dadi hundred per cent right,' muttered Mirchi, gazing out of the door. 'Not one chutki sabut against that Velu but he bechara in jail. And Meera giving mountains of proof about Harsh sahib but nobody believing,' he huffed. 'Why? Because Velu poor? And Harsh Shenoy driving big car?'

Mrs Ghosh turned her guilty eyes to Mirchi, shocked by the mirror being held up to her. With a sigh she lapsed into silent introspection.

Making its way down the busy bazaar street, the rickshaw stopped at a red signal by the maidan where the children had met less than a month ago. Mirchi gazed out, recalling the day when he had run around excitedly with the bat that was to become a catalyst in their alliance. On the other side, Meera looked out at the beach by the evening lights, remembering how she had picked tins and bottles for Mirchi's scrap collection. So much had happened in just a few weeks!

Noticing the lane up ahead leading into Anand Nagar, Malhar's eyes fell upon the large billboard they had walked by a few weeks ago in search of Sarla. Another film star's face was stretched across it now; and he was telling the good people of Anand Nagar, that by simply slapping on his brand of hair colour they could transform themselves into style icons like him—in five minutes flat!

'The hair,' Malhar nearly jumped, as the image triggered a brainwave. 'The old man's hair! It was just like...like...the one Harsh uncle wore in the play—Valmiki!'

'Oi Maa!' Mrs Ghosh covered her mouth with her hand. 'I never realized!'

'His height, skin colour,' Meera pressed on, 'they match with Harsh uncle too. Of course the glasses were fake like the hair.'

Mrs Ghosh nodded, her eyes fixed hypnotically on the ticking meter. 'I now remember, they pulled Aditya out of that international school few months ago and put him in the local one. They didn't say why but I know it was because they were struggling to pay the high fees. I've heard Harsh and his wife having arguments about it from my balcony. Some months ago, they also fired a full-time house help they had...perhaps that was also to save on expenses...' her voice trailed off.

Mirchi's words had caused a shift, a re-calibration of sorts, lifting the fog that had clouded their thoughts.

'You know,' nodded Malhar, reminded of his favourite book, 'In *The Mystery of the Burnt Cottage*, the owner... he burnt down his own house so he could get the insurance money. The most unlikely of suspects! So I guess anything is possible.'

'But what do we do now?' asked Mrs Ghosh, as their rickshaw pulled into the gate of Customs Colony. 'It is not right to name him before the police. Can you imagine how painful it will be for old Mr and Mrs Shenoy? They've already suffered a shock, and just received the good news that the idol has been recovered. We can't drop this bomb on them now! Shenoy uncle has been suffering from chest pain.'

Meera let out a laboured sigh.

'Before we identify him to the police, we have to be absolutely sure,' Mrs Ghosh whispered, as they neared their building, almost as if Harsh could somehow hear her. 'Else it will cause an awful lot of embarrassment and pain.'

'But what about the embarrassment and pain it has caused all the others?' huffed Meera, enraged by the thought. 'Sarla lost her job and nobody hires her now. Velu was in the lock up—what about his reputation? His sister's wedding was called off. Murguan Anna's shop was ransacked. Does all that count for nothing?'

'Shhhhh...' Mrs Ghosh hushed a charged-up Meera as she paid the rickshaw fare. 'Let's go up and discuss this.' She looked around as if she were about to steal something. 'Even if what you say is the truth —it must be tested.'

'But how are we going to test it? asked Malhar. 'Obviously, he is not going to own up to it!'

'He will!' Meera crossed her hands as her eyes fell on a line of post boxes in the lobby of A3. 'Come, I have an idea!'

50

The Trap

Tongue sticking slightly out of his mouth, Malhar cut hurriedly into the newspaper headline.

'Why do you need to do it like this?' tutted Mrs Ghosh. 'Just type it on the computer, print and post.'

'No,' Malhar set down the two words he'd cut out from the newspaper—*know* and *done*—and added them to the others in the plate. 'This is how Fatty would have done it.'

'We haven't got CONFESS yet,' Meera mumbled from behind the open page of a newspaper.

'What kachra you peoples making.' Mirchi tossed about the mountain of paper-cuttings on the table.

'Just wait and watch,' Meera squeezed glue behind each of the cut-out bits in the tray.

'You know Byomkesh Bakshi called himself Satyavenshi, meaning truth seeker,' said Mrs Ghosh. 'He was not driven by a desire to punish the guilty, but to discover the truth. After all, the criminal justice system itself has a dual purpose to punish and to reform. So after this, it doesn't matter what the Shenoys decide to do. They may decide to pursue the case or to withdraw their complaint to save their son. That is not in our hands. But at least they will know the truth.'

'Got it!' Malhar spotted the one word that was missing, cut it out and dropped it into the tray.

Mrs Ghosh handed Meera a plain white sheet to stick the pieces. 'Who is going to slip it under Harsh's door?'

'Main!' Mirchi volunteered. 'You both cutting and sticking. Me postman.'

'Cool,' Meera pasted the last of the cut-out words. Then held the page out for everyone to read the message.

'WE KNOW WHAT YOU HAVE DONE!
CONFESS TO YOUR PARENTS TONIGHT.
OR ELSE WE INFORM THE SSP IN THE MORNING.'

51

Closure

Two yellow eyes stared out of a crevice from the tamarind tree outside the Pradhan home as the resident owlet prepared to begin its sorties in search of dinner. Four brown eyes stared out of a window inside the Pradhan home as Meera and Malhar kept their gaze pinned on the stairway between the second and third floors of the A3 building opposite their bedroom.

'I don't think he's fallen for it,' Meera clicked her tongue. 'It's nearly eleven, doesn't look like he's going to speak to his parents.'

'What if he's called them on the phone?' said Malhar, dialling his art teacher from his grandmother's mobile.

'You think?' Meera bit her nails. 'This is too big to discuss over the phone. Especially when he lives right above them. What if he hasn't seen it yet?'

'He may take the lift down...'

'For one floor?'

'Ghosh aunty,' Malhar tapped the speaker button on the mobile. 'You saw anything?'

'No,' Mrs Ghosh's voice cackled through. 'I've been sitting at the balcony for over an hour. Haven't heard a thing.'

TRRRRR... TRRRRR... TRRRRR...

The doorbell made them jump, as the owlet whooshed silently over the window to descend upon a scurrying rat.

'Who can it be at this hour?' they heard Aaji muttering in the next room.

'Someone's at the door,' whispered Malhar. 'Aunty, we'll speak later.'

Hanging up the call, the siblings stepped out of the bedroom.

Aaji was hobbling towards the living room. Their mother was already there, standing by the half ajar door. 'No, Danny isn't back home from work yet,' she said to the person outside. 'He usually comes late. Can I do something to help?'

The other person's reply was inaudible. Meera and Malhar stepped closer.

'Please come inside.' Madhavi Pradhan threw open the door, revealing an anxious Harsh Shenoy rubbing the back of his neck with his handkerchief.

Meera pursed her lips. *Gilderoy Lockhart looked deathly pale!*

Malhar felt like punching his fists in the air. So he may not have been allowed at the raid, and his parents' decision to protect them may have robbed him of all the attention he rightly deserved, but the final act of the drama was to take place right before his eyes! What more could he want? They exchanged knowing glances.

'Can we speak in private?' said Harsh Shenoy, his forehead beaded with sweat. No *good evening* to Mrs Pradhan. No *hello* to the children. No *namaste* to Aaji. Nothing at all today.

'Yes, of course,' Madhavi Pradhan gave Aaji and the children a nod, then led Harsh to the sofa and switched on some more lights.

Aaji returned groggily to her room, muttering something about the unearthly hour. Meera turned back as if she were going to her room, then stopped at the end of the corridor and ducked behind a large bookshelf. Malhar crouched by her side, trembling with anticipation.

'I'm sorry to bother you at this hour,' they heard Harsh mumbling almost incomprehensibly.

'What's the matter?' Madhavi Pradhan's voice was soft but firm. 'Let me get you some water.'

'No, please, not needed...I...actually I wanted to speak to SSP Pradhan but I suppose I can talk to you as well, given you are a lawyer.'

'Yes, please tell me. What's happened?'

There was a long pause. Meera's heartbeat quickened. Malhar wiped his sweaty palms on his shorts.

'It was me!' Harsh broke the silence, a distinct quaver in his voice.

'Sorry…I didn't follow…'

'I stole the jewellery and cash!'

Silence from Madhavi Pradhan.

Muffled sobs from Harsh.

'Yes!' a thrilled squeak from Malhar.

'Shh…' a reprimanding jab from Meera.

'I…uh…I'm not quite sure I understand you correctly,' mumbled Mrs Pradhan.

Sobbing. Whimpering. Sniffling. Harsh.

Silence.

'Last year, I suffered a big loss in a new business venture,' Harsh finally spoke, his voice shaking. 'One of my shops was under mortgage. I defaulted on my home loan. I tried managing but…' More sobs and snivels. 'But there was no other way. I needed the money. I thought perhaps…'

Silence. And the whirring fan.

'I don't know what to say.' Mrs Pradhan's voice was soft, her tone flat.

'My business took a big hit during the pandemic.' Pause. 'I was under a lot of pressure… My mind wasn't working.' Pause. Snivels. 'When I saw all that jewellery my mother brought home from the locker, I just thought.' More sobs. 'It was rash. Impulsive. A terrible mistake.'

Silence.

'When I realized how much that idol meant to my mother, and it began affecting my father's health, I wished I could undo it all. But it was too late.'

'I...uh...can understand how hard this must be for you but what made you come here to confess all of a sudden? Do...do your parents know?'

'Not yet but I will tell them. I received this note today...I don't know who sent it. But I have already put my parents through a lot. I don't want the police turning up at my door in the morning and give them another rude shock. I thought it's better that I surrender and inform them on my own.'

'I see,' Madhavi Pradhan cleared her throat. 'As a lawyer, I must tell you Harsh, that you need to go to the local police station with this. But any confession you make before them will not be valid in court. You will have to make a statement of confession before a magistrate. And also, legally, you are not obliged to give evidence against yourself.'

'It is very late. I don't want to trouble my parents now...but I will tell them in the morning, after which I will hand myself over at the Sikkachowki Police Station. Could you please inform Pradhan Sir not to send the police? Will you tell him that I will surrender?' Harsh's voice was stoic and firm.

'I don't think my husband has any idea at all about this note but yes, I will tell him.'

'I feel better now, like a large stone has been lifted off my conscience.'

'It takes a lot of courage to own up to one's mistakes, Harsh. You did the right thing by confessing.'

Getting up from behind the bookshelf, Meera slipped silently back into her room. Malhar followed his sister, closed the door and began jumping. 'We did it! We did it, Didi! Look Fatty...I did it!' He held his favourite book to his heart then began dancing with it around the room.

Meera plonked down on the edge of the bed, filled with mixed feelings, happy to tick off the first of the puzzles they set out to solve.

Mystery of the Stolen Jewellery - √

Mystery of the Missing Idol- √

Mystery of the Vanishing Gods - √

Sometimes, the truth lies concealed behind layers of deceit. Sometimes, it stays hidden in plain sight. But rarely does it stay buried forever. Because the truth, like sunlight, always shines through!

52

Back Home

No vast crowd or grand procession would celebrate the return of the lord to his abode. Only some marigold flowers strung across a stone balustrade, two elegant brass diyas flanking the floor like sentries, and a selected gathering of attendants. For how does one formally restore an object, which has never been officially robbed? How could a thing be returned when it had not been removed?

'I am retiring next month,' said Mrs Sahasrabudhe, after they'd all spent many silent moments gazing at the statue of the ardha-nareeshwara at the stepwell. 'I was hoping to have the idol back before winding up but I was beginning to lose hope. You children descended upon me like manna from heaven! I can retire now without any regrets.'

Everyone clapped, then posed for pictures beside the stunning sculptures, to capture the special moment for posterity.

'I am reminded of that famous Hans Christian Anderson story, "The Emperor Who Wore No Clothes",' smiled Mrs Sahasrabudhe, stepping closer to the children. 'Sometimes, we adults are so caught up in a web of lies and deceit, we need children to break that bubble and call out the naked truth. I am most grateful to you Madhavi, to your two intelligent children, and to you dear boy,' she patted Mirchi. 'Your child,' she turned to Mirchi's family, standing coyly to the side, 'is pure gold.'

Mirchi's father pressed his palms together. Conscious, his mother pulled the pallu of her saree over her face. His grandmother beamed. His sister giggled.

Mr Murthi ruffled Mirchi's hair as they ascended the steps of the well. 'With both our children now in college, Paromita was getting depressed—you know, empty nest syndrome and all that. Now our Mirchi has filled that gap. He's been coming home to learn to read and he's a quick learner.'

Malhar gave Mirchi an encouraging arm-punch; Meera held up both thumbs.

'That's fantastic,' SSP Pradhan turned to Mirchi as they emerged onto the sunlit courtyard. 'I hear you want to be a policeman when you grow up...'

'Police...' Mirchi said shyly, bending to rub Munna under his neck, 'or Virat Kohli!'

'That's good,' the SSP patted the boy. 'It's good to have dreams but you must get back to studies. Now that you have Mrs Ghosh helping you to catch up, when school reopens next week, I'll take you there on the first day in my car.' He pointed to his official vehicle in the parking lot. 'Then we'll see who calls you dirty and who mocks you for being a sweeper's son!'

Mirchi's eyes twinkled as they fell upon the sparkling white police van. BHARAT SARKAR was embossed in bright red letters on its bonnet. ON GOVERNMENT DUTY stamped across its windscreen, red light on its roof. If he showed up in school in that chariot, even the school principal would treat him like royalty! A smile lit up his face.

'How presumptuous of me,' SSP Pradhan gave Meera a gentle tap on her head, 'telling you to keep your heart and mind open. The three of you have shown us how much is possible if only we adults can tear down the walls we build around us.' Mrs Pradhan nodded in agreement, touched by the friendship that had sprouted between the children, cutting across so many class barriers.

Meera held her father's hand, feeling silly about the fears that had confounded her. Seeing men like Shevre and Yadav and Pasha had planted a deep sense of distrust in the police. But the force also had officers like her father! She felt so proud. 'Thank you, Baba,' she pressed his hand.

'Thank *you*!' the SSP threw an arm around the three children. 'In wanting to help a hapless woman and an innocent plumber, you have ended up preserving our national heritage! So we all,' he pointed to everyone in the small circle, 'should be giving thanks to the three of you!'

'It's M4 actually,' Malhar rubbed Munna's sides, as the dog purred in contentment.

'Indeed,' smiled SSP Pradhan. 'Well done, M4!'

End Note

THE LAW

This story throws light on some aspects of Indian law, as also police and court procedure in India. While the provisions discussed in the story reflect the legal position when the book was published, readers should be aware that laws are territorial and change over time. Further, this book is a work of fiction for young readers, and is not intended to be a reference on Indian law.

IDOL THEFT

Those interested to read more about the problem of idol theft in India can refer to the book *The Idol Thief* by Vijay Kumar, and the *India Pride Project* that traces idols stolen from India's temples, and works with international law enforcement agencies to bring them back home. Visit Vijay Kumar's blog *poetryinstone.in* for more information.

YOU CAN HELP TOO!

As you read in the opening quote at the start of the book, India's art heritage is vanishing at an alarming rate—one thousand pieces per year/three per day.

The next time you visit an ancient temple or monument, you can do your bit by documenting it through photographs, videos, drawings, blog posts, articles. Who knows; if something goes missing from there in the future, your documentation may become a key piece of evidence in identifying the sculpture during legal proceedings to bring it back. Check *India Pride Project* to learn more.

Acknowledgements

Thank you Appa, for passing on to me a love for books, mystery books in particular, and interest in the law. Thank you also for being amongst the first to read the story and provide detailed inputs ranging from legal to grammatical.

Thank you Kabir, for being the first little reader of the series, and for encouraging me to keep going.

To Shilpa Chheda, Professor, Mumbai University and Heras Institute, St Xavier's College, Mumbai, I am grateful for the many informative and delightful tours of historic monuments in India. The trip to Rani-ki-vaav (Queen's Step Well) in Patan, Gujarat, and it's captivating beauty, forever etched in my memory, find expression in various forms, including through stories like this one.

Thanks Subhash Rao Mallya, for sharing stories and pictures of Mahalsa Narayani, the GSB community, and their past; and for recommending the book *The Goa Inquisition* by A.K. Priolkar which taught me much history. Thanks Anuradha Mallya, for a ton of information about the festivals and rituals of the community and their jewellery. Thanks Aparna Sambhare, for being my consultant on all matters Marathi. Likewise, thank you Rimi, for help with all things Bengali.

Thank you Vijay Hiremath, friend and advocate at the Bombay High Court, for being a ready-reckoner on matters of criminal law and procedure.

I also thank Vijay Kumar, idol-theft warrior, for his relentless pursuit of restoring idols stolen from India, and for penning the book *The Idol Thief*, which provided key inputs in my research.

Thank you Sudeshna Shome Ghosh, my editor at Speaking Tiger, for your faith in these legal mysteries and for signing on the series.

Always grateful to my family for their constant support and encouragement.

Coming Soon!

An M4 Mystery
BOOK 2

THE CASE OF THE Vanishing TURTLES

MALLIKA RAVIKUMAR

talking CUB
An Imprint of Speaking Tiger Books